THE BOOK OF

LAZARUS

ספר אליעזר

(Revelation Unveiled)

by

Dr. Allen E. Goldenthal

VAL d'OR PUBLISHING

ISBN: 978-0-6488083-6-7

4

LETTER FROM THE AUTHOR

What I'm about to discuss in the Book of Lazarus, is the assertation that the Book of Revelation was actually a Jewish prophetic book, an essential document of Hebrew apocalyptic literature, and that it had very little to do originally with Christian theology until it underwent considerable modification by the redactors of the Catholic Church. This will probably upset a lot of people on both sides of the equation. On the one hand, the Christian theologians will need to reassess their entire set of beliefs based on the Book of Revelation, since it is my intent to prove that the book's prophetic nature applies to our present particular time-period and has everything to do with the rising tide of anti-Semitism and the calls for the annihilation of the State of Israel, and practically nothing to do directly with the Christian concept of the Tribulation. Establishing how the promises for the end-time were made specifically to the faithful within Judaism, obviously will not appeal to the wider Christian world expecting the second coming of Jesus and receiving God's blessing for their remaining faithful to Christian doctrine.

For many Christians that will be a hard pill to swallow but to the Jewish religious community, the pill will be even much larger, as here was a book, obviously written with the intent to be disseminated throughout the Jewish diaspora, that prophesizes the arrival of the Jewish messiah with such detail that we can certainly predict the timeline once the prophecies described are filtered through a lens of current events. Simply because it was incorrectly labeled as a Christian text at some point in the late second or third century of the common era, the rabbinical authorities chose to ignore it and keep it from the Jewish population. We can blame the Rabbinical councils in the process of writing the Talmud for this decision, because they made the statement that Malachi was the last of the true prophets and there would not be another prophet until the Messiah arrives. One merely has to look in the tractate of Berakhot to find this seemingly unwise and profoundly discouraging decision. Superficially, one might think they made the decision based on some religious passage they found in the Tanakh, but the more likely reason was the advent of a prophet, or prophets threatened their self-proclaimed designation as the true arbiters of God. For two thousand years, Jewish homes have prayed through the common refrain, 'Next Year in Jerusalem', with the expectation that the Messiah would come at any time, but in the meantime any hope of there being a prophet had been negated by these rabbis. Essentially, they were making the decision for God, and because of my Karaite background, I will never forgive them for their sin of pride and self-glorification.

Here was a book, Revelation, if only it had been recognized for its Judaic connection, that at least would have informed the people that the Messiah will only come when certain conditions in human history were met according to its prophetic code. The book provides a highly detailed agenda, including a series of events that must take place initially, before we arrive at the End of Days. Clearly, possessing such foreknowledge would have prevented many that had abandoned the Jewish faith over the last two millennia, doing so because they lost hope after the Messiah's failure to come in their time of need. It is much easier to abandon one's faith when you can no longer believe in a religious organization that lacked an answer, when they asked the question, "When will the Messiah come to end our suffering?" It should be expected. Why would anyone believe in religious leaders that say they speak for God, but clearly, God does not speak to them. That was a misconception that they, themselves created, when they failed to recognize that God still has his prophets, and those that are true prophets have never stopped speaking for Him. Here was a book that provided a definitive answer regarding the arrival of the Messiah, readily available in Hebrew and Aramaic, obviously written by a Jew, for Jews and because of Jews, which would have at least provided some hope in knowing that the Messiah would be coming, but just not now. To those that had given up, considering it easier to assimilate into the other nations rather than hold on to what appeared to be a never-ending unanswered plea, I can only hope that when you hear the clear message in Revelation, that someday you will return to the faith of your ancestors.

Revelation is a Jewish apocryphal text and deserves to be taught as such. But after two thousand years of being referred to as a Chistian document, it would be hard to accept it as anything else if it retains that title. Therefore, I have renamed it as the Book of Lazarus, which will make sense to the reader once they have read this book and recognize that Revelation will be dissected to such a degree that it will leave practically no doubt in anyone's mind that it was always intended for a Jewish audience. The arguments for the retention of the Book of Revelation, also known as the Apocalypse of John, by the Christian churches will be heated as they have viewed this book as one of the most enigmatic and symbolically rich texts of the Christian New Testament. It will be hard to part with something upon which so many traditions and sermons have been based. But I will make a compelling argument that Revelation is undoubtably more accurately categorized as a Jewish apocalyptic work rather than a Christian one. My perspective is supported by the book's literary style, themes, and historical context, which align far more closely with Jewish apocryphal literature than with the theological focus typical of early Christian writings. For example, the literary style of Revelation shares significant similarities with not only Jewish apocalyptic literature, such as the Books of Daniel, Enoch, and 2 Esdras, but also with established and accepted prophetic Tanakh books such as Ezekiel and Zechariah. Apocalyptic literature is characterized by its use of symbolic visions, angelic intermediaries, and a focus on the cosmic battle between good and evil, all of which are prominent in Revelation. The vivid and often surreal imagery used, such as the four horsemen, the beast with seven heads, and the New Temple of Jerusalem, are all hallmarks of Jewish apocalyptic traditions. Moreover, the structure of Revelation is reminiscent of Jewish apocalyptic texts. As is a characteristic of the Book of Daniel, the Book of Revelation is divided into a series of visions, each revealing a portion of the divine plan for the End of Days. The use of numerology, particularly the significance of the number seven, is a key feature shared uniquely within Jewish apocalyptic writings. It should be noted that this symbolic use of numbers is less prevalent in any of the other New Testament texts, suggesting Revelation always had a much closer affinity with Jewish, rather than Christian literary traditions but this went unrecognized for a variety of reasons.

Furthermore, the themes present in Revelation specifically point to its roots in Jewish apocalyptic thought. The central concept of a cosmic struggle between the forces of good and evil, culminating in divine judgment and the ultimate triumph of God's kingdom are the cornerstone of Jewish prophetic literature and absent from other Christian texts which maintain that by spreading the Gospel, through the love of Jesus, mankind will be united and saved without any need for a final battle. This particular theme of a cosmic struggle can also been seen in the Essene community's book the War of the Sons of Light against the Sons of Darkness, depicting the faithful minority as being the persecuted Jewish population awaiting divine intervention through the Messiah to vindicate them and establish God's reign on Earth. The story in Revelation is not about a messiah that has come and gone, with the expectation of a return at some later time but depends on the actual destruction an obliteration of an evil empire with little sympathy as would be expected from a preacher of love. This very un-Christian theme is prevalent throughout the entire story, and as I will point out in this book, the insertion of Jesus's name several times by later Christian editors does not change in any way the plotline of the horrendous numbers of people slaughtered in battle.

It should be obvious to any reader to any reader of Revelation that whereas Christian texts refer to the spread of Christianity across the world by receiving Jesus's message, this book's main concern is the restoration of Israel through a "New Jerusalem". A New Jerusalem as the ultimate destination for the righteous of the Jewish nation is deeply rooted in Jewish eschatology as can be viewed in Isaiah 65:17-25. The vision of a restored Jerusalem, where God dwells with His people, reflects the hopes and aspirations of Second Temple Judaism, which longed for the re-establishment of Israel's glory and the fulfillment of God's promises to the patriarchs. At the time of Jochanan, those that survived the onslaught of Jerusalem by the Romans were already praying for the rebuilding of the Third Temple. Hence, the vision as detailed in Revelation aligns more closely with Jewish messianic expectations than with the early Christian focus on the spiritual kingdom of God that transcends earthly boundaries. Revelation's New Jerusalem is purely physical and earthbound city that suggests that whatever adulteration was done to the book to insert Jesus's name less than twenty times were performed much later, clearly in an effort to give the book at least a small degree of Christian authenticity.

The historical context in which Revelation was written further supports the argument for its classification as a Jewish apocryphal text. Revelation is believed to have been composed during the reign of Emperor Domitian (81–96 CE), a period of intense persecution for both Jews and Christians within the Roman Empire. However, the language and symbols used in Revelation would have been more familiar to a Jewish audience than to a predominantly Gentile Christian community. For instance, Revelation's references to the "Synagogue of Satan" and the importance placed on the tribe of Judah and the lineage of David indicate a much stronger Jewish context. The book's heavy reliance on Hebrew texts for its imagery and symbolism suggests that it was addressing a community steeped in Jewish traditions and expecting a messianic deliverer consistent with Jewish eschatological hopes. Additionally, the book's emphasis on the preservation of Israel and the role of the twelve tribes in the end times aligns with Jewish expectations regarding the return of the lost tribes, rather than Christian theology which claims no connection to any Hebrew tribal lore. Whereas Christian aspirations were increasingly focused on the inclusion of Gentiles into God's covenant through Christ, the focus of Revelation on Israel's redemption suggests that it was written with a Jewish audience in mind, one that was grappling with the implications of Roman oppression and being absorbed into the milieux of Gentile domination.

The fact that Revelation was adopted by the Christian community highlights the fluid boundaries that once existed between Jewish and Christian thought and practice in the first century. But over time, the separation of these two religions, through prejudice and the insertion of the governing bodies of Rome's Caesars such as Constantine to control and determine the direction of the Christian Church meant creating a distinct divorce of Christianity from its Jewish origins. What is amazing is that a book such as Revelation was adopted by the Christian canon in the first place, when it clearly was Jewish apocryphal literature, but the warlike nature of the book would have definitely appealed to the rulers of Rome that considered themselves to be destined to be the absolute rulers of a New Jerusalem.

To those Christians that read this book, it is not my intent to alienate you from God's prophecy or to discourage you from practicing your faith. The fine line that separates Judaism from Christianity should never be viewed as a barrier that prevents people from extending a hand of brotherhood between us. After all, Jesus did say in Matthew 5:17 that he had not come to abolish the laws of Moses (the Prophets) but to fulfil them. He was speaking specifically about adherence to Jewish laws. Certain statements made in this book may be construed as being anti-Christian, and I should make it clear at this point, that I do not believe in the deification of any man. That is the fundamental difference between Judaism and Christianity. But in saying that, as those that have read my book *The Caiaphas Letters* can acknowledge, there is no doubt in my mind that Jesus, as a historical figure, was one of the great Jewish teachers of his time, who's philosophy and teachings absolutely did change the world. That is indisputable, but where Christianity has placed their emphasis on the Man-God, I personally see his true value in his teachings and words. A man willing to die for his beliefs and possessing the ability to see the good in everyone, even those that may not have deserved it. In my opinion, making him more than a man serves only to lessen the value of what he represented.

So, as we read this book together, both Jew and Christian, it is my hope that together we do not only perceive the prophetic message with clarity but that we also find a solution together to avoid the incredible devastation it has predicted. It is the description of the final war which makes it possible to overlay what is written with recent world events, that tells us that between now and the year 2050, the world today will very like be the subject matter of the book and if ever we wanted to take responsibility to avoid the destructive and fatalistic events of the prophecy, then now is the time we attempt to make a difference. We must recognize that a prophecy is intended to tell us what will happen if we make no attempt to change or stop the process as it is unfolding. That means we can control our own destiny and that of the world, if we consciously stop ourselves from moving in the current direction as depicted in the prophecy. If we choose not to, then the prophecy will be fulfilled. God does leave us with a choice, even though the current madness of our world would make us doubt that we have the ability to do so. We can remain silent and let the world unfold as it is, or we can rise up together to stop the impending doom and create a better world without suffering through the evens of the prophecy. Hopefully we will make the smart choice.

Dr. Allen E. Goldenthal

1

INTRODUCTION

To those of you familiar with the Book of Revelation, it should be immediately recognizable that this book is completely different from all the other books in the New Testament as it is prophetic in nature, describing a time in the future where there will be incredible suffering and death before the believers in God are delivered from the End of Days and mankind is finally permitted to live in peace. This is in contrast to the Gospels and letters, which instruct the followers to embrace Jesus and they will all be saved. No such promise exists in Revelation. In fact, in comparison to the other New Testament Books, with the removal of the few references to Jesus that exist in the book, one would mistake this book as just being another prophetic book of the Old Testament, spreading doom and gloom. A companion book to the Book of Zechariah which talks about the same subject matter.

Whereas the books of the New Testament are generally focused on the events of Jesus's lifetime, describing the miracles that were attributed to him, along with his preaching and strongly emphasizing the belief that Jesus would make his reappearance during the lifetime of his apostles, The Greek version of Revelation makes no attempt to even suggest his reappearance will come anytime in the near future and in fact, any suggestion of a reappearance might be at the very End of Days should he be that Messiah that is being described riding on a white horse. But for the purpose of this book, I will be relying on the translations from the Aramaic Peshitta version of Revelation, which is very different from the various translations that circulated as the Greek versions. My argument being that Jochanan, the John in the Greek translations, would have written in either Hebrew or Aramaic. Therefore, the Peshitta is far more likely to bear a resemblance to the original manuscript, unlike the much later Greek translations.

If we are to even assume that any references to Jesus in the Book of Revelation are authentic, then we must question why such a significant player in the faith of the apostles would only be mentioned 14 times in total in the Greek translations of Revelation, with almost half of those references being in the first nine lines of the first chapter. More to the point, the first five mentions appear to be obvious insertions, as they appear to be intentionally provided for no other purpose than to give Jesus some role in the text, because an examination of the structure of the sentences would suggest that his name was not there originally. And that reality is confirmed from the different versions of the Aramaic translations in which his acknowledgement ranges from practically not being mentioned to not at all, depending on the Aramaic version cited.

As we attempt to read the very first sentence as it may have been originally written in the very first Aramaic manuscript, *'The Revelation which God gave unto his servants to show things which must come to pass'*, then we can see how it was possible for a later editor to easily insert the phrase 'of Jesus Christ' afterwords and the word 'shortly' to accommodate the editor's belief that Jesus had to be the intermediary and how Jesus was expected to return 'shortly' as per their beliefs. The book clearly points to a distant future and it must be noted that there is no doubt from the sentence structure that it was God's angel that was sent directly to John and the story was never related or revealed by Jesus to his apostles as is being suggested in the later Greek translations. But the most striking evidence that the Jesus references were inserted much later is the use of the words Jesus Christ whenever there is a direct reference to God, as if to say, 'don't forget Jesus too,' as not only does this make a clear distinction that Jesus was not God, but not even the son of God, but only a 'messiah' or 'anointed one' as the word Christ infers, without any of the other deification attributes. But whereas we had come to the belief that God would only speak to the people through an intermediary such as Moses or his select prophets in the Old Testament, the book of Revelation clearly states that the angel delivered God's message directly to John and it would be his responsibility to deliver it, suggesting that he was in the eyes of God at a comparable level to any of the other Old Testament prophets. It was this direct line of communication that obviously troubled the later Church editors because it meant that God could still deliver messages without involving Jesus, relegating Jesus to being non-essential, and furthermore under such circumstances, Jesus could not be considered as being the last prophet or messenger as the Christian faith emphasized. As a result, these editors felt compelled to insert Jesus as the intermediary, even though the structure of the sentences definitely states otherwise.

Sentence five of the first chapter of Revelation is an interesting one as we can see from the flow that it was originally part of sentence four and the original text would likely have read as follows: *'From John, who is the faithful witness and the first begotten of the dead and the prince of Kings of the Earth, to the seven churches which are in Asia; Grace be unto you and peace from him which is, and which was, and which is to come, and from the seven Spirits which are before his throne.'* This particular reference to an everlasting God, existing at the beginning, the middle and the end of time is strictly Old Testament, as is the throne reference with the spirits. More importantly,, the sentence serves as a vital clue that there was more to John than being merely a common man and in all likelihood he was the follower of Jesus that was called Eleazar in Hebrew, or Lazarus in Romanized society. The giveaway that this sentence was pertaining to John as Lazarus and not Jesus is the fact that he says he was the first begotten or the first to have arisen from the dead. As we know from the New Testament, Jesus was the last of his group to arise from the dead. The first one within in his inner circle was Lazarus. This is the first indication as to why I have decided to call this the **Book of Lazarus**, but as will be detailed later within the chapters to follow, there are many more reasons to suggest that John or Jochanan was most likely Lazarus and the one referred to as the beloved disciple. Lazarus, the same follower who gave up his own anointing oil to have his sister anoint Jesus with it. But again, all this will be explained once we delve deeper into the book. As Lazarus was likely a descendant of the house of David, thus having his own tomb within the outskirts of the city of

Jerusalem, not to overlook the aforementioned sacred anointing oil that he was in possession of, he would be recognized as the Prince of Kings, because his Davidic heritage was the eternal line anointed by God. This divine right of Kingship was later usurped by every royal family in Europe afterwards, claiming to be God's anointed, which is why we see Dei Gratia on many of the coins from countries that still have a monarchy, but the truth is they weren't selected by God at all, and all of them will just crumble into the dust of ages as time passes, fading from every one's memory. As to why this claim arose among the European monarchies, I suggest you read the book, **Blood Royale.**

As a royal descendant, then who is Jochanan or Lazarus writing for? Most prophets inherited the spirit or mantle from one of the earlier prophets. Ezekiel donned the mantel of Moses, Zechariah that of Ezekiel, and it is clear from his style that Jochanan inherited the mantle of Zechariah. Each subsequent inheritor adds to and embellishes the nature and visions of his predecessor. As the name Moses, apparently stripped of its royal attribution when restored to its original Egyptian derivation, but translating as 'the son of' in the ancient Egyptian language, it can be seen that Ezekiel fills that absent name with one of his own choosing, calling himself 'the Son of Man', a representative of humanity. The mantle is then picked up by Zechariah, the son of Berechiah, the son of Iddo, where Iddo most likely means the one that is now the 'continuation' and therefore it was likely Zechariah's way of suggesting his father was Zerubbabel, the crowned royal that was now the continuation of the House of David after the exile. Therefore, Jochanan is stating his right to claim the mantle, because he too, represents the continuity of the Royal House of David. When we search though the Book of Revelation, to see whom Jochanan or Lazarus is directly delivering his message to, it becomes questionable if he is even concerned about the followers of Jesus, now known as either Mineans, Nazoreans or Christians, depending on their location and ethnic background.

This book is not intended for those of the Jewish faith or nation to question the foundations of their belief structure but instead, to recognize that although the books of the Tanakh, are all sacred, they do not represent the sum total of books that could have been incorporated into the texts of Judaism. The prophets, wisdoms and psalms were selected over a two-to-three-hundred-year period of time, as the self-declared esteemed leaders of the Jewish people, known as the wise tannim, the amorim, who considered themselves to be infallible, determined what their congregation should and should not read. Like all men, they were guilty of human vanities and selected what supported their personal belief structures and rejected everything else. Only through negotiation, common interest, and selecting those books that weren't offensive to any particular party or doctrine did the texts now constituting the Old Testament, manage to make it safely through the process and are accepted as being divinely inspired. Unfortunately, this meant a lot of other books of highly significant value to understanding Jewish beliefs and Hebrew origins never made it through the screening process. Some of these we still can find as the Apocrypha, or Pseudepigrapha, others have been lost forever. And in the case of the Greek translations of Revelation, some have been so radically edited by other denominations that they can no longer be recognized for their inherently Jewish doctrine.

For those of you of the Jewish faith that believe that the Tanakh is complete and exactly as it was intended to be, and that the selection of books was divinely inspired and therefore cannot be tampered with or questioned, then this book will probably be upsetting for you to read as I will present justification as to why *The Book of Lazarus*, entitled Revelation in the Christian New Testament, is more likely a Jewish Apocalyptic book that was specifically overlooked during the formation of the Tanakh because of its direct relationship with one of Jesus's apostles. It is a marked failure of Judaism to negate anything and everything associated with Jesus simply because his preachings, which were inspired by the Hebrew scriptures became corrupted by others much later, and what should have been the insights and teachings of a great Moreh during the Roman occupational times, instead became a polytheistic and somewhat idolatrous theology as a result of those that wrote long after his departure from this world. If we exclude texts such as the books of Enoch, or Jubilees, or even some of the books found in the Dead Sea Scrolls such as the War of the Sons of Light with the Sons of Darkness, simply because the aforementioned team of self-appointed rabbis made it their responsibility as to what should and shouldn't be included in the religious content of Judaism, then we in fact have negated some of the most enlightening and spiritually relevant writings of Jewish heritage.

According to this premise, it is my intention to demonstrate and explain why *The Book of Lazarus*, also known as Revelation, is one of the most significant Jewish prophetic books of our time. This in turn will challenge numerous Christian theologians to attempt to try and reclaim this book as part of their justification for their belief in the return of Jesus at the End of Days, but as will be clearly explained, when those fourteen references to Jesus, which were not even cleverly inserted into the prophecies are removed, along with the several lamb references, also clumsily inserted, then what remains is easily recognizable as a prophecy that pertains specifically to the Jewish people and the land of Israel, in accordance with the prophecies already accepted in Ezekiel and Zechariah.

The significance of *The Book of Lazarus* is that it speaks to our present time in human development and history. This is not my first discourse warning of the coming Armageddon, but all my bewailing regarding the crumbling nature of our society, our families, our beliefs was never going to change the world, because all the Judeo inspired religions have made the conscious decision that there will be no more new prophets. This decision is totally against God's mandate in which he will send prophets as needed and never put an expiry date on this particular heavenly policy. If God is eternal, then so must be his intention to forewarn and inspire mankind whenever it veers off from its intended path. And since mankind will always be fallible, then so too will be the need for prophets to aid us in our survival. But since none of us, it would appear intends to dissuade a world determined to seed its own destruction by proceeding in the direction it is heading, then it is necessary to turn to the most relevant prophecy from the past that speaks of our current time, so as to be forewarned.

It was several years ago that the leaders of our free world agreed that Iran should have nuclear power, which actually means nuclear weapons, because that is exactly what their agreement achieved. These world leaders would like us to believe that they can delay such a possibility for years, but as I write this book, the achievement of the goal of a nuclear weapon by Iran is only weeks or months away. But then the world leaders, as seen in the recent media believe that the Mullahs of Iran will have an epiphany and come to the realization that they don't need to destroy Israel, nor will they attempt to eradicate America. Not only is this attitude naive in its thinking, but it is also ashamedly ignorant of reality. Combine this seemingly unstoppable development with the international global market beginning to teeter, while financial advisors talk the catch phrase of market correction, and you can be pretty certain another recession or depression is around the corner. Align the above issues with the quagmires in both the Ukraine and the Middle East and it can only spell disaster.

As the most recent executive branch of the United States for the past three and a half years has managed to turn Black against White, poor against rich, woman against men, the LGBTQ+ community against two-gender believers, Gen-Z against baby boomers, and confused the boundaries of morality to such a degree that even unborn babies are being sold for cellular material with the financial blessing of government sponsorship that permitted until recently to allow abortions all the way to the end of the third trimester, then if ever the world was tottering at the edge of extinction, this surely is that time. If we permit it to be forced over the cliff edge, then the world as we know it or wish it to be, will be unrecoverable.

Therein lies the dilemma, because saving ourselves from the onset of Sodom and Gomorrah seems to be impossible. We have move too far past that point to press the reset button. Perhaps we cannot turn back the hands of time and correct this world of insanity with its amoral philosophy calling itself normal, and those that have a belief in normalcy being based in humane morality or religious tolerance classified as the ones who are abnormal because it is simply too late. What we can hopefully achieve is an agreement on the understanding that evil is a natural development in the absence of morality and as a result, it can become the accepted norm. Therefore, the evil that we have spawned through the abandonment of normal societal values and a Judeo-Christian morality that was once seen taking seed post-World War II, will run its course exactly as described within *The Book of Lazarus,* because we have closed our eyes and sealed our lips. We can only hope that some of us will raise our voices and take a stand that we no longer will accept the willful destruction of our society, the tearing down of our moral code, and the erasure of the truth by governments and media that do nothing but feed us lie after lie. If we can find that courage, then we may be able to pull ourselves back from the precipice. Admittedly, it is far easier to sit back and accept the former eventuality, than challenge the authorities as in the latter case, but then I must remind you that we have always been warned not to accept the smooth path. Remember that evil can only spread when good people remain silent. Our choice; our destiny; our future.

"Read the Book of Eleazar!"

"Who? What?" Pearce was completely confused by this point.

"That was my reaction as well," I acknowledged. "I knew of no book with that title. Caught me completely off guard."

"When did this happen?"

"It was a while ago," I admitted.

"So, what happened next," Pearce was eager to know.

It was funny I guess, that in all the years I have known John Pearce, he never changes. Not in his appearance, and certainly not in his personal habits. When he arrived at my home this morning, it was somewhat of a surprise, as this was the first time he never sent a message in advance to advise me of his coming. I was caught off guard.

"Exactly why are you here John?" I guess it was about time I asked him the question which had been bouncing around in my mind for a quarter of an hour.

"Because you called me, Doc."

"I never called you John. What are you talking about." That fact is that I almost never call John about anything because I know that any time I talk to him, he's going to pressure me for a new story.

"Sure, you did," he insisted.

"No, I didn't, John," I stated quite firmly. "And why would I? We just released *Vienna's Last Waltz*. Why would I call you so soon afterwards."

"I swear to you Doc, you called me. Said it was urgent, and we had to work on this next book right away. You even said the fate of the world depends on it."

Now I was completely confused. I may be getting older but I'm not that old that I could completely forget about a long-distance call to Canada to speak to John. "And I swear to you John that I never called you. What else did I supposedly say?"

"That was it," he replied. "Just to work on this new book right away, claiming the fate of the world was at stake and then you hung up."

"You're certain you weren't dreaming," I asked, knowing that he would deny it, but I had no other explanation as how he could have received a phone call from me when I'm almost certain I never made it.

"It wasn't a dream," he confirmed what I expected him to say. "But you just said that you heard a voice saying to read the book of Eleazar. Maybe you were dreaming and called me?"

"As if I was sleepwalking," I questioned him. "What would we call this, sleep-phoning? I don't think so, John. And if I did, my wife would certainly make me aware of it. She's a light sleeper. If I'm up, then she's up."

John just shook his head. "I wish I had recorded the call when it came through, but I didn't think it would be necessary."

"Maybe it wasn't…" I commented.

"Ungh…I don't get it," Pearce scratched the disheveled mop of hair on his head.

"Because obviously it was intended to bring you here and that can only mean that I am obligated to tell you what was revealed to me during this episode. I'm not being left any choice in the matter."

"A choice with who?" Pearce still didn't understand what I was saying.

"Hey, I was confused. And the more I began doubting that this voice was what I thought it was, the more confused I was becoming. I don't have a clue how you received a phone call from me but the matter of believing it or not was no longer left in my hands. I never should have doubted where the voice had come from."

That piqued John's interest. "You're suggesting that this was like the time when we were recording the events in *The Caiaphas Letters*. That it was coming from you know who."

"You can say His name John. Not as if you're going to be struck down. Especially not after receiving a phone call from Him."

"You're suggesting I received a phone call from God?" John asked, sounding somewhat flabbergasted.

"Well, you certainly didn't receive one from me," I responded. "But I guess He saw I was hesitant in writing about his at all and this way I would be forced to do so."

"A phone call from God?" Pearce was beginning to sound like a recording stuck on repeat.

"We've experienced a lot stranger things over the time we've known each other," I reminded him. "A phone call is pretty minor in comparison."

"Now I really regret that I didn't record that call. Just imagine what it might have said if I had call identifier."

"I would think it most likely would have said 'unknown caller'", I responded.

"You really know how to take the fun out of things, Doc."

"Don't worry about it, John. Just think about the fact that heaven has your number," I laughed at the thought of Pearce being on direct dial.

"Ha, ha, Doc. Very funny," he replied sarcastically. "Back to your dream or whatever it was. What were you told next?"

"You ready? Because once I start rolling with this story, I don't want to stop. So, you better have everything ready to go now."

Sitting with his pens and notebook in his lap, while he pressed the record button on the tape recorder, Pearce nodded that he was prepared to go.

"You sure? No coffee, no bathroom break?"

"Positive. Let's begin."

"Alright," I agreed and was about to begin when Pearce blurted out another question.

"Is this one of those stories where you tell me to just let you ramble on without any interruptions or are you going to let me raise questions while you recite your narrative?"

"If I say you can ask questions as long as you're not constantly interrupting my story, will that be acceptable?" I offered him what I thought would be an equitable arrangement. "Deal?"

"Yeah, deal," he agreed.

"You can imagine my state of mind. Here I am being told to read a book that I had never heard of before, and I could find no proof that it even existed. it was surprising to say the least."

"This doesn't sound much like GLEEM," Pearce clearly saw the difference when he made his observation. "I'm guessing this has nothing to do with ancestor's memories then."

"Not as far as I can determine," I assured him. "Actually, the name Eleazar was rarely used in my family, although I did use it for my oldest son's middle name."

"So how do you figure it then, Doc?"

Hard to believe that Pearce can be a columnist for a newspaper with such a masterful grasp of the English language. "Are you asking me what do I think?"

"Yeah, that's what I'm asking," he replied as if I should automatically understand Pearce-speak. After so many years of working together, perhaps I should.

"Well, I couldn't place the name through one of my ancestors but then I started thinking, what if it was a book that one of my ancestors was aware of and not actually their story."

"You're telling me this is some ancestral memory of a book they once read. Sounds a little farfetched if you ask me," Pearce gave his two cents worth of an opinion.

"Just for the record, I didn't ask you, I'm telling you it was a thought that flashed through my mind. And then I started calling myself a fool. Or perhaps it was that other voice in my head calling me a fool, but whichever it was made me think that the name may not have changed over time, but the language certainly would have. I thought if I Romanized the name then I would have Lazarus. But what would I, or at least one of my ancestors, have to do with Lazarus that I didn't already describe in *The Caiaphas Letters*? Even there I described Lazarus as someone who couldn't offer anything of value to enhance Judaism. As you're well aware with your Catholic upbringing, he was nothing more than a showpiece designed to glorify the mystical powers attributed to Jesus. But as soon as I thought that, then I heard that voice instructing me to read the book again. I realized then that I must be on the right trail, even though I still didn't know what I was looking for. Because even if this was about Lazarus, there's still no book in the New Testament by that name."

"Then that's a dead end," Pearce pointed out so poignantly.

"I thought so too until I started calling myself fool again, or at least that voice in my head was calling me that. So, while still talking to myself, I said, well if you want to play that game than let's do it. Eleazar or Lazarus like all Hebrew names has a meaning behind it. Translated from its Hebraic origin it means God Who Helps Me or God is My Supporter.

"And that was the answer to this mystery?" John asked.

"No, not at all," I rebuffed his assertion. "I was still in the middle of this translation game, and I knew it. So, I said to myself, what other languages are being spoken at this time? The answer was easy. Most of the people were speaking Aramaic and Hebrew was retained more for traditional religious services. I'm thinking now, if God is My Supporter, what would my Aramaic name be and it came to me. My name would be Jochanan, which not only meant God Is My Supporter but also God Who Graces Me. And if my name was Jochanan and I was living in the Roman world, what would they call me? The answer to that should be pretty easy for you, John."

"John."

"That's right," I congratulated him. "The Book of Eleazar must be related by some means to the Apostle John. And as you know, your New Testament attributes two books to him. One being the Gospel of John and the other being Revelation."

John adjusted himself in the chair, pulling on his trench coat which was beginning to bind his legs as he twisted and squirmed.

"Is that the same coat you wore thirty years ago when we first met?" I asked.

"Sure is," he grinned. "London Fog, it's a classic," he stated proudly.

"That's one way to describe it," indicating I wasn't too impressed. "Don't you think it might be time to retire that thing and get yourself something a little more modern?"

"No way, Doc. This coat will never be out of style."

"Well take it off, or something. All your fidgeting is interrupting my though process."

Pearce agreed to strip off his trench coat and lay it over the back of his chair. "Is that better?"

"Definitely! Now at least I can concentrate on what I was trying to tell you. Where was I?"

"The Gospel of John."

"Right. I was telling you I narrowed it down to either that book or Revelation that I was being told to read. From the onset we know that the Gospel of John is unique in that ninety percent of its material can't be found in the other gospels."

"That's a good thing, right?" John was curious as his Catholic school upbringing kicked in.

"Not necessarily. From sentence fifteen in Chapter one, you realize that the writer of this book considers himself to be John the Baptist. And therein lies the problem, because if he was John the Baptist, he was executed long before Jesus was and therefore, he couldn't possibly write about all the events in Jesus's life that occurred after his death. Remember, John the Baptist was executed around 29 AD. Jesus wasn't crucified until four years later."

"Are you saying that John didn't write the Gospel of John?" Pearce sounded a bit confused by my insinuation.

"Oh, it starts out fine as if it was written by John the Baptist but by Chapter Five sentence thirty-five, we are made aware from the context of Jesus statement that John had been executed by that time. John is described as a lamp that had burned and gave light but now Jesus says he has taken over that role as the season that John had been preaching and baptizing had come to an end. From that point onward, the style changes dramatically and there are no longer any reference made by John to himself as was typical in the first three chapters. And chapter ten is the icing on the cake because whoever took over writing the gospel, wrote in sentence forty and forty-one the following: "Then Jesus went back across the Jordan to the place where John had first been baptizing, and he stayed there. Many came to him and said, "Although John never performed a sign, everything he said about this man was true." From these two lines we can see that John is dead and buried, but people still remember what he had said about Jesus.

"And your point is…" Pearce obviously didn't appreciate my commentary on one of his sacred gospels.

"Well, it could mean that the author of the book is a liar and was not the original John the Baptist that appears to have started the gospel, but overlooking that simple fact, we realize that this new author claiming to be John is very knowledgeable regarding certain events in the life of Jesus. What I find most interesting is that Chapters 11 and 12 are primarily concerned with Lazarus and his sisters. Lazarus's death, his resurrection and his having a feast at which his anointing oil is used to anoint Jesus. The most significant statement is in the first sentence of Chapter 11. 'Lord, the one You love is sick.' Lazarus is identified as the 'beloved disciple' of Jesus. What also is made clear is that the other disciples were not particularly fond of Lazarus. Unlike them, Lazarus represented wealth, affluence and was held in high regard by the general populace without revealing exactly what his position in society actually was. And since as I explained that the names Eleazar and Jochanan were interchangeable, depending on the language being spoken, the author that took over as pseudo-John, may have been Jochanan and he wrote quite a bit concerning Lazarus because he was Lazarus!"

"How do you figure that, Doc," Pearce inquired.

"Figure what exactly," I wasn't sure what he was referring to.

"That he was rich and from high society." Pearce couldn't understand how I could deduce such a statement. Of all the conclusions I had just drawn, I found it fascinating that what concerned him most was my insinuation that Lazarus was rich."

"That's the easy part but one which most people don't have a clue."

"It's not that easy because I still don't have a clue," Pearce insisted.

"Judas provides the answer when he says the nard or perfumed oil could have fetched them 300 denarii or more. Do you have any idea how much 300 denarii is," I threw the question out to John, who immediately shook his head. "That's why most people don't have a clue because they think of it as loose change in their own pockets. So, what if it can get them 300 silver coins, all about the size of a dime. When you think of it like that, then it would seem like they're talking about thirty dollars in today's money. That's a bit better than pocket change but still not enough."

"You're going to tell me it's a lot more than that, aren't you Doc?" Pearce picked up on my intimation.

"Want to take a guess at it John?" I provoked him.

"Er, maybe a few hundred dollars' worth?"

"Let me explain it to you this way. Twenty-five denarii would be the equivalent of a gold aureus. That being the case, then the oil was worth twelve gold aurei. That's not cooking oil we're talking about. Not even candle oil. It is far more valuable. Rome used the aurei as its standard costing for three centuries in that one aureus would get you four hundred liters of wine, but if you weren't a drinker then one aureus could also buy you ninety-one kilograms of flour. So, twelve of them would set you up as a merchant of wine or flour quite nicely. We're talking a lot of money!"

"That oil was worth quite a bit," was all that Pearce could say.

"You think? It was a phenomenal amount of money and they were just pouring it out on Jesus as if it was water. You can only do that if you were so rich that it didn't matter if you wasted a fortune."

"And this is important because…?" Pearce still didn't get my point.

"Because this voice in my head wanted to make it perfectly clear that this Lazarus wasn't just anybody; he was somebody special, and he was the key to whatever mystery I was to unlock. Let's face it, he had a sepulcher in the aristocratic district of Bethany, a suburb of Jerusalem. That area was reserved for only two Houses in Judaism. The House of Aaron and the House of David and he's clearly not from the former in this instance."

"And now you got it figured out," Pearce supposed.

"The references to Lazarus in the Gospel of John are usually in the third person and in the past tense, which suggested to me that this book was written by someone who knew him well but did not necessarily agree with him or even like him, but was still afraid to deny Lazarus his prominence in the events of the time. Besides having money, which would not be enough reason for the author to have this attitude towards Lazarus, there had to be something in his genealogy that made him superior to the other apostles. As I have already explained in *The Caiaphas Letters*, that happens to be his genealogy. Being of the Davidic line gave him instant credibility and authority, but as he ran naked from the Garden of Gethsemane and his subsequent failure to testify on behalf of Jesus only led the others to revile and despise him. Hence the question when they ask Jesus how long is this despised disciple expected to live, hoping that he would die soon or they could execute him for his failures but Jesus's reply that if he wanted this individual to live forever, what business was it of theirs. That response by Jesus was very revealing.

"Maybe to you Doc, but I'm still not getting it."

"He indicated that Lazarus was somebody special, someone that all the other apostles were expected to defer to. He's pointing me towards Lazarus the same way that voice in my head was doing."

"Aha." I think it was beginning to dawn on Pearce what I was driving at.

"There had to be a book that this voice was pushing me towards. There was only one book that has always been attributed directly to John or Jochanan, who now you can appreciate was Lazarus. It just happened to be a book that I once criticized, saying it looks like it was written by a man on magic mushrooms. Now I have to sort of eat those words if I'm being told subconsciously that I need to pay attention to it."

"That book," Pearce said with a deep breath.

"Yes, that one," I concurred. "I think I'm being told I have to reveal the truth about Revelation."

"You're saying that this Book of Lazarus is what I grew up knowing as Revelation."

"That's exactly what I'm saying John. He pretty much tells you it's so right at the start of the book."

"But the other gospels don't really say that much about Lazarus. He's not even listed as being one of the apostles."

"That should have been your first hint that something was up," I advised. "How could someone so prominent be so absent at the same time, especially considering how much time Jesus spent in Bethany. The Gospel of John clearly tells you that Lazarus was the one that Jesus loved the most. And in Revelation, he tells you with complete certainty that he was the 'beloved disciple.' How could that be and at the same time he's overlooked by all the others. One can only conclude that they intentionally wanted to conceal anything to do with this Lazarus fellow. It should be obvious that there was something they were afraid of that they didn't want their followers to know about him. Only in the Gospel of John, which I remind you was a very late gospel, written almost half a century later than the other ones, does the importance of Lazarus become highlighted as if someone was trying to correct an intentional oversight."

"Yeah, but you're still talking about Christian dogma, Doc. Doesn't matter what you call him or say about him, it's still about Jesus."

"Are you sure about that," I challenged his faith.

"I mean, it was taught to me during my days in Catholic school. I don't think they would have done that if they didn't think it was about Jesus."

"I don't really think they knew what they had," I responded. "And that's why I think I was being challenged to look at it.'

"Challenged by whom?"

"That is the question, John. Maybe, it's our mission to find out."

"You think that's why you called me?"

"It may be why you're here but I'm telling you again John, I didn't call you."

"So how do you explain the call?"

"By now John you should have realized that there are some things that defy explanation." I was exhausted having to make excuses about a call that I don't believe I ever made.

"Especially when it comes to you Doc," Pearce laughed.

CHAPTER TWO: THE REVELATION

"It is a strange book when you first look at it," I commented. "Incorporating much of the prophecies from Isaiah, Jeremiah, Ezekiel, Daniel and Zechariah. In fact, at first glance, one might even accuse the author of plagiarizing most of his imagery from these earlier prophets."

"Except he talks about Jesus," Pearce interdicted.

"Not really," I corrected his mistake. "According to your version, he only mentions the name Jesus Christ fourteen times in a book that's twenty-two chapters long. And most of those mentions are in the first chapter."

"Ah, yes, but he talks much more about the lamb of God," Pearce was quick to point out in one of those Gotcha moments he was desperate to catch me in.

"Yes, twenty-eight times to be exact," I agreed. "A lamb with seven horns and seven eyes, which are the seven spirits of God. Doesn't sound much like Jesus to me. "Not to mention the references to the wrath of the lamb. I'm guessing you were taught in your Catholic upbringing John that Jesus was all about love but that's not the case with this lamb. This lamb's about revenge! This lamb is vicious!"

"But whenever they mention God, they also say the lamb is present," Pearce defended his belief.

'Yet, God is on his throne and the lamb is apparently mentioned as an afterthought. I can easily replace most of the references to the lamb with the name Israel and it actually makes more sense. Remove all the times the books says the throne of God followed by 'and of the lamb' as if it was inserted afterwards and that becomes eight less mentions. Then there's also the three mentions of the marriage of the lamb, which according to the other prophetic works was usually a reference to God taking Israel as his bride and we're down to a mere seventeen references to the Lamb. There is actually only one clear reference to the lamb as Jesus and that's when it mentions the twelve apostles of the lamb."

"Well then, one should be good enough," Pearce explained in his typical irrational logic.

"Except even that reference doesn't make much sense, saying the names of the twelve apostles are inscribed on the twelve foundations of the city. Not on the twelve gates because those had the names of the twelve tribes of Israel inscribed on them. One enters the city through its gates. But the twelve foundations, it would appear that the fact that they were supposed to refer to the twelve apostles is quickly forgotten and they're just made of semi-precious stones five lines later. So much for any reference to the apostles."

"Why couldn't he be saying the apostles were like precious jewels to be cherished," Pearce still couldn't accept the possible error in his thinking. "That's how I would interpret it."

"Who were the twelve apostles John?"

"That's an easy one Doc. There was Peter, Simon the Zealot, John, Matthew, Andrew, Philip, Thomas, the two James, Bartholemew, Jude, and…"

"Come on, says it John, give me number twelve."

"Well…reference to the twelve was just a common expression."

"Don't weasel your way out of this John, say the name of number twelve."

"Judas Iscariot," he finally admitted reluctantly.

"Now, do you really think that someone would write that one of the foundations of this New Jerusalem was built on the foundation provided by the essence and spirit of Judas Iscariot, the man who betrayed Jesus and made his execution possible for thirty pieces of silver?"

"Twelve was just a number that they commonly threw around at the time," John tried to sound convincing but knew he was fighting a losing battle.

"Not in a million years, John," I ridiculed his statement. "That's why I'm pretty sure the reference to the foundation layers being related to the apostles was a later addition and an erroneous one at that. The original version I'm certain only talked about the twelve semi-precious stones but some later editors saw an opportunity to Christianize the story but made a mistake that no one seems to pick up on, even two thousand years later. Either you accept that Judas's spirit is an equal contribution to the soul of New Jerusalem, or you need to admit the reference to the Apostles of the Lamb was a later addition. Take your pick."

"Why would they do that Doc?"

"Because it was a deliberate attempt to try and tie the prophecies of this particular book directly to Jesus, through numerous references to the Lamb in order to dissuade any follower of Judaism from seriously looking at the book."

Pearce looked confused. "What possible reason would they have for trying to keep the book out of Jewish hands? They actively sought Jews as converts."

"Quite simply, the book claims that in the future the Jews will be restored as God's beloved children and their capital city will be rebuilt and from it, God will reign over the world. Everything that the Christians believed was going to be delivered to them is turned one hundred and eighty degrees into a promise to the Jews, and this is being said by Jesus's most beloved and trusted apostle. It confirms the prophecies of the Old Testament and the promise to the Jews. Do you think that Christian clerics would want that message delivered to the Jews at the same time they're trying to convince their own congregations that the way to forgiveness and heaven was only through Jesus? The book is actively promoting everyone to be Jewish. If the book was recognized as Jewish apocrypha, it could have been the death knell for the early Church. They had no choice but to modify it if they were going to keep it as part of the New Testament."

"So why now?" Pearce still found it hard to accept. "Why two thousand years later are you trying to make an argument that the book should be restored to its Jewish heritage."

I had to laugh at his insinuation. "I could say to you, better late than never but I won't. And you're making the mistake that it's me trying to make an argument to justify the book's attachment to Jewish theology. I already told you; it was that voice in my head advising me that it would guide me through the book in seeing what was original and what had been added. It would explain to me the man behind the book, the offense he had committed against our God, and why he had been punished for his defiance. And in the end, it promised that I would see how the book was left for us to uncover its true origin, to understand its relevance to Judaism, to appreciate that it may be the most sacred and inspired of all our prophetic texts once the false additions intended for de-Judaification had been removed."

Pearce scratched the back of his head while listening to my explanation. "Hard to believe Doc if you keep referring to a divine inspiration as 'it'. Either it was a message from God, or it wasn't. You can't have it both ways."

"It was a presence in my head John. I can't assign it to being male or female. I can't tell you whether it was angel, God, or Lazarus, himself. If I refer to it as 'it', that is only because it was non-corporeal, manifestation out of the ether, and therefore it was genderless."

"Non-binary?" Pearce attempted to make a joke out of it.

"Not funny, John!"

"I still don't see why now! Why didn't the Jews accept it back in the first century when it was written before all the Christian editors had an opportunity, as you claim, to alter it?"

"I don't think I ever said we rejected it straight out," I challenged his assertion. "Some would have immediately rejected it simply because of the author. I think Caiaphas mentioned that nothing good ever came from the House of Lazarus in my book *The Caiaphas Letters*. That would have been enough to turn some in the Jewish community away from reading the book, but I believe others did read it and then mistakenly acted upon it."

"Acted upon it? What is that supposed to mean Doc?"

"There are always those that believe they can make prophecies unfold, rather than let them happen naturally. They want to force them into reality. The Bible is filled with people trying to intentionally fulfil prophecies but repeatedly failing. I believe the miracle of prophecies only occurs when the events happen beyond our control, and we have no other choice but to accept that God made them happen."

"How exactly did certain people attempt to make the prophecies in Revelation take place?" Pearce was curious. "That's what you're insinuating, right Doc?"

"I think certain people read the book and that is why they attempted to revolt against Trajan in 117AD and then later on against Hadrian in 132 AD. They believed that they could not only win these wars but restore Jerusalem because they had a book that prophesized they would do so."

"But those wars were disasters," Pearce emphasized the last word.

"You can understand then how we would have rejected this book after it led us into to the Bar Kochba war because men like Rabbi Akiba misinterpreted its prophecies, thinking it was meant for his time, but instead it sealed our doom and the expulsion of hundreds of thousands of Jews from the Holy Land. A rejection that made all of us refuse to pick it up again, leaving it for the followers of Jesus to embrace it as their own after they made certain corrections to its content."

"Guess the book would have been seen as more of a curse than a blessing in that case," Pearce admitted, having accepted my point as a possible explanation.

"This may all sound pretty extreme, and I know it will be a hard pill for you to swallow, considering your Catholic upbringing, but it is a distinct possibility. In fact, I'm still having difficulty in dealing with this personal revelation, hence my avoidance to write about it right away. But that avoidance has only resulted in what I consider some personal punishments and now I can't avoid it any longer."

My last comment piqued his interest. "Punishments? What punishments exactly, Doc?"

"Nothing major," I assured him. "Nothing I won't recover from."

"Does that mean you're not going to talk about it? Pearce tried to press me further on the issue.

"That means I'm definitely not saying anything more about it John.

"So, you intentionally held back on telling me about this when it first happened," Pearce pursued the conversation from a different angle. That's the reporter in him, working hard to dig out a story.

"I may have delayed talking about it immediately, but it wasn't all entirely my fault."

"How so, Doc?"

"I was told that I would know the time was right when it was clear that a friend was clearly a foe. That's the main reason I sat on it for so long."

"And this friend became a foe just now," Pearce inquired.

"Oh, he was dancing around the issue for a long time," I informed him. "In fact, he was so wishy washy that it was hard to tell actually what he was saying. That didn't help me to determine when the time was right either."

"Just so we're on the same page here Doc, who are we talking about?

"I'm referring to the Democratic party in America, John. You didn't like me using the word 'it' so I referred to it as 'he'. The party used to be a strong supporter for Israel and against anti-Semitism but became nothing but a clown show on the second night of the Democratic National Convention, filled with the most overwhelming tidal wave of hypocrisy that could ever be manifested. That was my clue. A so-called friend was definitely a foe at that point."

"I thought you would have liked what they had to say, Doc. The night, as I saw it, was intensely Jewish oriented. You had Emhoff and Schumer directly discussing their strong connection to the Jewish identity and then you had Bernie Sanders and J.B. Pritzker take the stage. And don't forget they opened the night with an invocation by

Rabbi Sharon Brous. I would have thought that would have made you at least a little happy that they were supporting the Jewish cause."

"Like I said, nothing but a pandering clown show. Did you notice that absent altogether were any references to the inexhaustible U.S.-Israel alliance. Once upon a time that was a staple of Democratic politics. Not one word by Shumer about Israel. And let me tell you about these clowns, just so you know how much they disgust me. Rabbi Sharon Brous unfortunately lives in a fantasy world and has no understanding of the reality that faces Israeli's every day. She spoke of a future in which Israelis and Palestinians "live in dignity and in peace," but how does she think that will happen when the charter of the Palestinians calls for the elimination of Israel and the death of Jews. Does she have a magic wand that she intends to wave and change reality. I think her speech last October during Yom Kippur sums up her views best. Here she was warning against racism and religious extremism in the "increasingly hardline, ultranationalist and what she referred to as the messianic government of Israel that she believes threatens the whole project of the state of Israel, and less than two weeks later Hamas invaded Israel and slaughtered over twelve hundred Israelis. Who were the extremists and racists in that case? How many times has she condemned Israel and given a pass to the real problem, which it the fanaticism of the death cult among the Palestinians. And how dare her refer to Israel as a project as if it is some homework assignment that she has taken home from school to work on. Israel is not a project; it is God's will and promise to his Chosen People and anyone that refers to it as a project doesn't have a clue about the essence of Judaism."

Pearce held up his hand in a defensive posture. "Calm down Doc. You're going to give yourself a heart attack at this rate."

"Let's be realistic, John, she calls her congregation non-denominational which means she has absolutely no affiliation with any official religious group. She can be affiliated with some Satanic cult for all I know, disguising herself as quasi-Jewish congregation. Do you know who the greatest enemies of the Jews have been throughout history, John?"

"The Nazis?"

"No. The greatest enemy of Jews have been Jews. Self-loathing; fearful of being identified; hating that they are separated from the majority of the people in the world; desperate to assimilate Jews!"

"Is that how you see her then," Pearce questioned my perception.

"She's an appeaser. She bathes in the approval of those like her and the non-Jewish communities because she preaches a message of universal love which they see as an opportunity to sway her to their side."

"But why does their have to be sides at all, Doc?"

"You actually ask that question after being raised in the Catholic doctrine? How do I get to enter heaven John?"

"What do you mean?"

"You know very well what I mean. It was a simple question. How do I get into heaven? Now answer the question."

John hesitated because he knew his religious doctrine very well. "Through the acceptance of Jesus as Lord."

"Well fortunately I believe in the Shekinah and not in heaven, otherwise you've already cast me into hell or purgatory, because I will never accept Jesus as Lord. The reality is that there have always been sides and there is no such thing as universal acceptance. We're friends John, but that single doctrine in your beliefs will stop us from being brothers, because in the end, we both see the other condemned to a different eternity. Do you understand now why I called the DNC a hypocritical clown show?"

"You see her as one of those self-serving Jews that seeks the love of everyone else and would betray her own people to achieve that goal."

"Yes, I do. Having her there was strike one supporting the friend becoming foe comment. And then they offer up Bernie Sanders as representative of the Jewish people. A devoted socialist, that makes atheists look like they're choir boys at a local cathedral. The man even admitted that politics is his only religion. Strike two regarding friend becoming foe. And then there's good old Doug Emhoff, Kamala's husband. What can you say about a man that admits he only began feeling his Jewish roots after he found himself married to the vice president, whom he attends church with, where there is a reverend that is openly hostile to Israel. Emhoff admitted that most of his life, Judaism played a very small role in his life but now he stands on a soap box and says, *'We know the freedom that my family members and that American Jews everywhere have yearned for and championed, the freedom that our nation promises to all of those that live and worship here, that freedom has at times been undermined by hate. As my wife, the vice president, Kamala Harris, would say, we must speak the truth about that. We must speak truth about this epidemic of hate. American Jews and Jews worldwide have experienced and continue to experience hostility, discrimination and violence.'* And then his wife goes out of her way to say the Palestinians and the protesters have a point, as they're attacking Jews in the streets and the workplaces, never being arrested or condemned for their acts violence. Why, because they have a point that she truly believes in. There you go, strike three for the night, which definitely confirmed to me that friend had become foe."

"But Doc, there were a lot of Jews that think it was a very pro-Jewish night. And don't forget Pritzker came out very pro-Israel."

"One out of five, John. Even Schumer, who once claimed his name came from the word, "shomer," meaning a protector and therefore he must be a guardian of Israel, never even mentioned the events in Israel once during his entire speech. You want to know how bad it is? Go read my book *America's War Against The Jews* and then you'll know why it was clear to me that now was the time."

"Maybe you can give me a copy if you have one lying around," Pearce suggested.

"I'll check but I'm surprised you haven't even read it yet."

"It was on my list."

"Sure John. Like Christmas is marked on my list of things to remember."

"Well, if you give me a copy it will definitely be on my list," Pearce grinned.

"If you want it that bad then I'll wrap it up and it can be your Christmas present," I informed him.

"Geez, that's so kind of you," Pearce commented sarcastically.

"You asked for it, that's what you'll get," I laughed.

CHAPTER THREE: END TIMES

"After reading the book, it became clear to me why this voice urged me to read it. I could recognize that it was Jewish in origin, a unification of the various and sometimes conflicting messages of our recognized prophets. It was Yahweh's final warning on the events of our time, events that no matter how much I thought could be avoided, it was never possible and like Sodom and Gomorrah, all that is about to occur was always intended to occur. Not even Abraham's pleading could stop it."

"That sounds pretty ominous," Pearce commented. "You're suggesting it can't be avoided.

"No, I'm saying if we don't do anything about it, then it's going to happen," I corrected him"

"But you just said it is about to occur and was intended to occur."

"Let me explain it to you John. We're both walking in a forest and I see a cliff ahead but you don't see it and you're heading straight towards it. At the pace you're moving at, you are going to go right over the edge in a matter of seconds. I have two options. I can yell for you to stop immediately, thereby saving your life, or I can say nothing and watch you go sailing into the canyon of oblivion. A prophecy is a warning, no different from me yelling for you to stop. But even after I scream for you to stop, it is up to you as to whether you do stop or keep walking over that cliff."

"In that case, you're hearing this message was in order for you to find a way from stopping the prophecy from being fulfilled," Pearce surmised.

"Either we must strive to avoid the disaster and if not, then at least be a warning of how we may, just maybe, will be able to survive the coming apocalypse."

"So why have a prophecy for our present time, delivered to someone two thousand years ago? That makes no sense to me at all," Pearce applied his 21st Century logic.

"It does if you accept that time is meaningless to God. We measure time in reference to our lives, but what if you're immortal. Time really has no significance then; it simply passes, and we endure it. From Jochanan's time to us may have passed like mere seconds in God's existence."

"But we're not immortal," Pearce protested. "Time is important to us and can't be ignored."

"On an individual basis, you're right. You can't afford to squander that much time because you want everything within your lifetime. But as Jews, God did present us with the gift of immortality in that he would protect us and see that we continue to live on, no matter what evils cross our paths, attempting to eliminate us. Three thousand two hundred and fifty years and counting; thirty-seven hundred if we count from the time of the patriarchs. And as you know, over those four millennia, there have been numerous attempts to erase our existence. Yet here we still are. As a people, a race, a specific ethnicity, we do have this appearance of immortality and therefore two thousand years is a mere drop in the bucket."

"I get what you're trying to say Doc, but two thousand years, really? It's still a heck of a lot of time."

"Answer me this John; you believe Jesus is going to return, don't you?

"Yes."

"Originally, they thought it would be in two weeks, then it was two months, followed by two years, two decades, two centuries and then finally it became two millennia and in the year 2000 everyone was standing on mountain tops waiting to receive him. But he didn't return, did he?"

"No," Pearce shook his head regretfully.

"So, as I understand it, you're still waiting for him, and I have no idea what the next time period after two millennia is called but you're still waiting no matter what. Therefore, explain to me how a two-thousand-year prophecy that is strictly Chrisitan is okay but if it's a Jewish one, you perceive it as being too long and not credible."

"I guess there is no difference," he concluded.

"Right answer," I congratulated him. "Whether we call him Eleazar, Lazarus or continue with Jochanan, the fact that he was selected to be the messenger during his time and deliberately avoided and shunned this heavenly assigned task, preferring instead to have another, being his close friend Jesus, take up the mantle turned out to be a big mistake because everyone assumed the message was about their own time. Ultimately, in the end, after Jesus was dead and his followers had split Judaism, fragmenting it into a group known as Mineans, Lazarus realized that his abdication of responsibility proved to be a colossal mistake and he finally had to accept the role that was given to him. But it was too late and now he had no other choice but to present his mission in the form of a book before the turn of the first century. After all that he had done, there were very few of his own people that were going to listen to him or trust him if he merely preached the prophecy."

"But you said the Jews used the book to support their wars against Trajan and then Hadrian," Pearce jumped at the opportunity to try and catch me in an error.

"No, I said some of those in power, like Akiba used it to justify instigating a war, but as you would have read in **Beneath A Falling Star**, the man had his own personal reasons for starting a war that would practically destroy Israel."

"So, he's another Jew that you blame for turning his back on Israel."

"Who, Akiba?"

"Yes, him," Pearce confirmed.

"I don't even consider him to be a Jew. There are ten commandments and he broke practically every one of them."

"That's a pretty serious accusation to make."

"Add that book to your reading list as well and see if you don't agree with me after you're finished, John. But let's get back on topic regarding the book of Lazarus. John probably sat on the prophecy for years, releasing it at a time when he saw trouble around the corner but couldn't say definitively that it was worse than what he had witnessed in the past. Whatever may have been his reasoning for doing so, he released it."

"What is whatever the case supposed to mean. Wouldn't he have been around when Titus destroyed the Temple? What was he witnessing almost thirty years later that could have been worse than that."

"The disintegration of his own body, perhaps."

"I don't get it," Pearce failed to grasp my meaning.

"I told you that years before the other disciples questioned how long would they have to put up with John's presence. You know that story where Jesus tells them, "If I want him to live forever, then what is it to you." Well, it was beginning to look like that was more of a prediction than an off—the-cuff comment. John would have been well over ninety by the time and probably looked and felt every day of his age. Having a long life isn't worth it if you're suffering at the same time and I'm betting that he began thinking he was being cursed with this longevity. Potential immortality in a decaying body would be worse than a life-long prison sentence. A curse that he must have thought could only be broken when he released the prophecy that he had been carrying around for seven or so decades."

"What are you basing his age on," Pearce questioned.

"He was a companion of Jesus, so most likely born around the same time, and it's pretty well established from the references he uses in the book that he could be talking about none other than the Emperor Domitian, whom he reveals had died, and that occurred in September of 96 AD."

"That all?" Pearce still wasn't accepting what I believed to be reasonable facts.

"Are you saying that's not enough proof. There's more if you want then," I answered smugly. It always bothered me when Pearce would question the historical facts I presented to him. I think it's a disease common to everyone working in the media today. They refuse to accept facts if they don't agree with their own beliefs and then go out of their way to find some biased fact checker to negate what you've told them. "I guess you might believe your own Church theologians, such as the commentaries from Victorinus in the 3rd century. He tells us that Lazarus clearly felt he had to suffer for prior sins and his exile to a small Greek Island was part of his punishment but upon the death of Domitian he felt absolved of his crimes. A curious comment when you first examine it. What sins could Lazarus possibly have committed that he had to be exiled for?"

Pearce started humming and hawing as if I expected him to provide an answer.

"That was a rhetorical question John, I'm about to answer it for you. We know from the writings of Flavius Josephus that Vespasian had his sons Titus and Domitian round up all the prominent Jews in Israel an exile them around the Empire as punishment. With the death of Domitian, he probably felt as if he could finally return from exile, but to what exactly would he be returning to. It must have been clear to Lazarus that he bore some responsibility for the fall of Jerusalem, the destruction of the Temple, and the death of perhaps half a million Jews during the war against Rome as a result of the things he did or didn't do. As long as the House of Flavius was on the throne in Rome, he held himself accountable. With the death of the last Flavian Emperor, murdered actually, Eleazar probably felt released of some of this guilt."

"How can you say that he was in some way responsible for the first Roman-Jewish War?" Pearce obviously objected to my insinuation. If he was going to continue to challenge everything I said, then this was going to be a very long day.

"In the same way I can suggest that the Mineans or early Christians were responsible for the death of the King Agrippa. His murder was the catalyst for the war twenty years later. Had Agrippa not been poisoned, he would have kept a united Judea and Galilee within the empire as a friendly satrap that the people would have found acceptable. It wouldn't have been perfect, but believing they were being ruled by their own Jewish king would have significantly reduced the influence for those clamoring for a liberated Israel."

"And you believe that the Christians murdered him," Pearce questioned more than making a statement.

"I have no doubts. "The Romans would have been delighted to finally have a peaceful reign arise in the Jewish provinces. The Jews, for the most part, relished the thought of having a king that was more Hasmonean than Herodian. They would have viewed it as a restoration of the Maccabees. There was only one population that would be unhappy, because they were promised that Jesus was the last of the Jewish kings and he would be coming back to sit on the throne. To them, Agrippa was an obstacle to that return, and he had to be removed. All it took was someone in his royal staff being a Christian and slipping him a drink with poison in it before he took the stage that day. But once he had been murdered and Rome decided not to put his son on the throne as a replacement, then things began to get very ugly in Israel. It was a ticking time bomb that didn't take Nero much to push it over the edge."

"So, you're saying that was all John's fault," Pearce I could still tell objected to the comment that Lazarus knew that by extension of his role as a disciple, that he indirectly was responsible for the destruction suffered within the provinces.

"Not only did he feel responsible, but he also knew that by withholding the release of his prophecy at that time, his visions had they become known may have convinced many that this was not the right time to go to war and in all likelihood, Israel would be destroyed, which it was." I don't know how I could make it any clearer to him.

"And by the turn of the century he suddenly knows that it was the right time. What would make him think that?"

"Not exactly but he knew he was running out of time. He had lived longer than most and even though the Gospels suggested he would continue to live until such time that Jesus said it was enough, I believe he clearly understood that he was not immortal and that the time had come to depart this world and end his suffering. He communicated that the battle of Armageddon would take place only after his passing and it would be a time for the cleansing of all the sins of his people and a restoration of Israel. And I believe it was a mistaken expectation that it would happen soon after his passing that prompted the rabbis to encourage the revolt in 117 AD against Trajan and afterwards led Akiba to believe that his was the next generation predicted by this prophet Eleazar or Lazarus. Sadly, Akiba was not only wrong, but the Bar Kochba war put a nail into the coffin of our nationalistic hopes for quite a long time and resulted in the expulsion of even a larger number of my people throughout the empire."

"That was a pretty big nail," Pearce tried to make a joke of an extremely tragic war. "Its aftereffects lasted for 1800 years."

"Not quite," I corrected him. "More like two hundred years."

"What the heck are you talking about Doc?"

"Most historians have no clue when it comes to Jewish history, John. They are under the misconception that somehow Hadrian expulsed all the Jews from the provinces, and we were all wandering the earth for the next eighteen centuries until the UN approved the creation of the state of Israel in 1948. That's absolute crap. We were always a substantial presence in Judea, Samaria and Galilee, even if the Romans wouldn't let us call our homeland that, and created a new name for the territory, calling it Palestina."

"Any proof of that Doc?"

"I wouldn't say it, if it wasn't true, John. The fact that we were still the dominant population in the land was evident when we decided to go to war against Rome for a fourth time?"

"Fourth time?" Pearce repeated my words somewhat shocked.

"Yes, a fourth time and it was known at the Gallus Revolt because it erupted during the Roman civil war of 350–353, when Constantius Gallus was sitting on the throne as Caesar in the eastern half of the empire. In 351–352, the Jews of Roman Palaestina, oh how I hate that name, revolted against the rule of Constantius Gallus, brother-in-law of Emperor Constantius II. Sadly, once again we lost, and the revolt was crushed by Gallus' general Ursicinus. But obviously we were a large enough population to raise an army against Rome and that should put an end to these ignorant historians that keep insisting that Palestina was depopulated of its Jewish indigenous people."

"That's good to know Doc but what does all that have to do with what was written in Revelation?" Pearce couldn't see the obvious connection.

"It's about the controversy," I tried to explain to him. "There are two ways you can view a prophecy if you see it as a promise of better times. You can either just let it happen or you can try to make it happen. The latter approach resulted in three very bad outcomes for the Jews because they assumed the prophecy was all about their struggle against the Roman Empire and couldn't see anything beyond that. You can't make a prophecy happen. You can try to stop it, if you don't like what it entails, but if you don't, then it will happen. You just don't know when because it involves all the pre-conditions being met. The Jews during that period covering three centuries didn't understand that because they became reliant on a rabbinical class that did all their thinking and interpretation of biblical prophecies for them. After three successive failures the rabbis distanced themselves from the book. But what was now considered a false promise within Judaism was picked up by Christianity and accepted as a promise of their kingdom to come. A perceived abandonment of God's selection of the Children of Israel as His chosen people, only to have that promise given as an inheritance to the offspring of Judaism, being Christianity."

"So, you're saying it was intended to be a Christian book after all."

"No, that is not what I'm saying. Where did you get that idea? What I did just say is that the misguided rabbinical class that now dominated Jewish religious life in what was once Israel, thought they could control the outcome of the prophecy, and they failed miserably. In the same manner that many believe they can control angels and destiny through their mystical works of the Kabbalah. More trash that has nothing to do with Judaism and should be eradicated, but that's another story. God works according to His own schedule. He doesn't measure his work in hours and days as mankind does. To do so is a human folly. Only when all the preconditions were to be met, would the prophecy take place. As such, no man has control of seeding those requirements in order to make them happen."

"Wouldn't one of those preconditions be the onset of Christianity?" Pearce inquired, his mind still refusing to accept that his book he had grown up with may be something completely different from what he was taught to believe.

"I think it might be best if I go right back to the beginning and put this all into its proper context," I suggested.

"As in the beginning of the Bible?" Pearce responded.

"Not that beginning. Lazarus's beginning. As I already said, in regard to his age, he was born around the same time as Jesus. Perhaps in the same year when the conjunction of Mars, Jupiter and Saturn occurred in the heavens, a conjunction that Jewish astronomers referred to as the Messiah Star. You know, the one you call the Star of Bethlehem. We already know that Lazarus was from Bethany, or at least his family had a large estate there just a couple of miles from Jerusalem, on the southwest side of the Mount of Olives, with a sepulcher, thereby indicating the prominence and significance of his family. A few more miles to the south lays Bethlehem, where Micah indicated the Messiah would be born. In Micah's time there was probably little distinction between the two places. Lazarus, as we know from the gospels, is in possession of the anointing oil. He is also referred to as the most beloved of Jesus's disciples, and his sister Mary bore the cognomen of Magdelene."

"Is that important?" Pearce wondered.

"Very," I answered immediately. "Magdelene, from the Hebrew word Migdala, translates as the Tower, a likely reference to the Tower of David from the Song of Songs. From this cognomen we can take several inferences. One perhaps that she was very tall, but unlikely. It could also be an indication of being a very powerful woman, and we have no reason to doubt that when we notice the other disciples actually seemed in fear of her and her influence over Jesus. Or we can take it at its most obvious reference, which is to the Tower or Family of David, since the song says that the shields of a thousand great men adorned the tower, indicating that she was of the most prominent of families, to which all of Israel had sworn allegiance. Essentially, we have a descendant of David, born in close proximity to Bethlehem, in possession of the King's anointing oil, born at the right time under the Messiah star, but deathly afraid to take up his responsibilities as this holy deliverer."

"This is beginning to sound like that Monty Python movie, the Life of Brian," Pearce suggested.

"There is a bit of a resemblance," I agreed. "What if everything was pointing to the likelihood that you were intended to be the Messiah, but you were too afraid to pick up the mantle and instead let someone else grab the limelight?"

"It would make things very complicated," Pearce responded.

"Yes, so much so, as I mentioned previously, the other disciples keep asking Jesus how much longer they have to put up with the presence of this possible alternative. Clearly, his existence was a contradiction to everything they professed and that bothered them greatly. Jesus knew that Eleazar or Lazarus had a special purpose and that he would not be released from this life until he fulfilled it but by this time, Jesus had been declared as the Christ and Eleazar was a complication. Only after Domitian's death, does Yahweh permit Eleazar to die, a fact emphasized by Christian authors when they write that Jochanan was a very, very old man when he finally was laid to rest. That was his punishment; a life in exile, a price on his head, and the knowledge that he failed to fulfill what God had expected of him because he ran from his responsibilities. In the same manner he ran from the scene at the Garden of Gethsemane, when Jesus was arrested, or as the story goes, fleeing into the night naked, having been stripped of his cloak. I don't know if it actually meant that he was physically naked. It may have been a metaphor, referring to his denial of Jesus as messiah, exposing his cowardice, and abandoning his own hopes that the Galilean would assume what was actually his personal mantle but which he was too fearful to accept."

"Or it could have been that he actually did run through the streets naked," Pearce interjected.

"Possibly. I can't refute that it was a factual statement but as a metaphor, it more accurately describes this concealed relationship that the Gospels go to great lengths not to talk about. In the aftermath, it is this abandonment of Jesus which causes the other disciples to question why he should be permitted to live to a ripe old age, according to the Gospels. If that was the case, then were they actually contemplating his murder because they would have no way of knowing how long he would actually live at that point in time? And if they weren't discussing murdering him, then that would mean that they were aware that he was someone quite special with a purpose far beyond being just a disciple."

"Just as a point of clarification, how do we know that this particular John is Lazarus? There was another disciple with that same name."

"A fair question. Christianity attempts to obscure it is Eleazar by confusing him with that other disciple, but that John happened to be boiled in oil around 81AD. But to think it was that other John requires the reader to ignore the fact that in Revelation, this Jochanan states clearly in his introduction that he is the disciple that Jesus loved the most. The so-called beloved disciple. But you know who else was a beloved follower of God, David. We know that David was God's beloved through several passages in the Bible that highlight his unique relationship with God. From the moment David is anointed by the prophet Samuel, we are told that "the Spirit of the Lord came mightily upon David" in 1 Samuel 16:13 and that despite his imperfections and sins, David was referred to as a man after God's own heart according to Acts 13:22. David's heartfelt psalms, filled with praise, repentance, and a longing for God's presence, further reflect the closeness of their bond. Even in his failures, God showed grace and mercy toward David, reaffirming His love and favor for him throughout David's life. As you can see, there is a drawing of a parallel here. David as beloved of God and Lazarus as beloved of Jesus. As a scion of the royal house, Lazarus is comparable or the equivalent in the relationship to King David."

"Aha!" Pearce jumped on my comparison. "And that would mean according to your own comparison, that Jesus is the equivalent of God."

"In the sense of a master and servant relationship, then you're correct John. You know I won't say that Jesus was the same as God, but in this particular example, he was the guiding master to Lazarus as the Almighty had been to David."

"But you implied it," Pearce pointed a finger in my direction.

"Are you really going to try and push this, John?"

"Most certainly," he quipped.

"What I've implied is that clearly, Lazarus knew he was the designated heir of the Davidic monarchy, and that he believed in some ill-conceived manner based on the prophecy that he was intended to overthrow the Roman yoke upon Israel and probably assumed incorrectly that with the death of Domitian, that the time had finally come for the liberation of the Jews within the Empire. If the Flavians, whom had been responsible for the destruction of the Temple and much of Jerusalem no longer existed, then surely that had to be a sign that God was ending Roman dominance over the Children of Israel. There would now be a cleansing of the earth and eventually a restoration. All those that had been scattered to the four corners of the Empire by the fall of Galilee and Judea would now be returned. Based on what followed, it was evident that the communities within Israel and those in the diaspora believed this to be true. As the Davidic messiah, Eleazar had finally delivered his message in the form of Revelation, and how could anyone doubt it to be true. After all, if he was the true heir to the throne of David, then his word was undeniable."

"Alleged heir," Pearce still refused to accept my argument.

"Even if just alleged, in order to prove him right, the Jews of Alexandria, Cyprus and several other provinces attempted to initiate the war and restore Jewish independence in 117 AD. Trajan swiftly put an end to that. Perhaps they argued that it wasn't the right time. The events that Lazarus had spoken of hadn't actually manifested as required prior to their attempted revolt. They decided they would wait until the book and events were more closely aligned. Fifteen years later, as I told you previously, they believed that to be the case. Four years of massive death and destruction which made the first war against Rome pale in comparison. Once again the restoration promised by Lazarus's visions failed to manifest and the Jews were made to suffer horribly. Then, as I describe it in my book ***Beneath a Falling Star***, the same rabbis that had encouraged the war effort based on the Book of Revelation now abandoned and cursed it. It was more a case of let the Christians have it with all its seeding of destruction, rather than Christianity inheriting it. But for the sake of good measure, the rabbis went ahead and placed a further curse on the House of Phiabi, because Ishmael the Second was a descendent of that particular priestly house that they now accused of having given them false hope in a briefly restored and consecrated temple. Rather than look at their own sins, they concluded the subsequent downfall could only have been the result of Yahweh despising the Phiabians as well."

"Isn't that the same priestly house that you said you were descended from," Pearce asked as he recalled what was written in my previous books.

"Yes, that is my House," I affirmed his suspicion. "As I describe in my book, not only was Ishmael part of my house, but the prosecution against Akiba was also led by an ancestor. It gave the rabbis good reason to hate my ancestors. They also point to the fact that Jeshua ben Gamaliel, the last High priest when the Temple fell to Titus was also from the House of Phiabi. Now that the same outcome had occurred when a member of that same house fell to Hadrian, then surely that priestly house must be cursed. And since that time, every Yom Kippur, the Rabbanites will stand during their recitation of the Amidah in their synagogues and curse my family."

"That sounds terrible," Pearce sympathized.

"If their curses actually meant anything, then perhaps it would be. To me, it's just water off a duck's back and I forgive them for their own arrogance. But back to Eleazar or Lazarus because, as I was saying, once Domitian had died, he was revived in his Judaic beliefs as if he had received his own personal baptism from God. He honestly believed that his prophecy could restore a Messianic hope to those survivors of the First Roman Jewish War. But what he did not realize was that the images God had shown him were never intended for his time, and therefore his words were never intended to save anyone. He was merely a messenger to pass on the revelations of our time, which are now unfolding before our own eyes."

CHAPTER FOUR: INITIAL VISION

"As I read the book of Revelation, as I already told you, it became quite clear to me that it had been heavily edited over time. But if you were to ask my opinion John, I'd tell you as an author that this editing had been done quite poorly. The original content is written in the first-person perspective, and both the style and of course the perspective are quite distinct from those paragraphs and sections that you can find written in the third-person. Not only that but you can find sharp breaks in the subject matter being discussed in order to interject a sudden reference to Jesus, which are completely out of context with the content and not even related to the subject matter being discussed. It's as if these editors were so afraid that the prophecies were going to be interpreted as non-Christian related, that they became desperate and inserting references to Jesus or the lamb wherever they could. Yes, that's the right word. Their insertions look like the actions of desperate men. Yet, the book still didn't lend itself that well for these insertions and that's why there are so few of them."

"I never noticed the switching before, regarding first and third person writing," Pearce scratched his head as to how he could have not seen that before.

"It even becomes more obvious with the addresses to the various Churches because you can see that they were penned by someone that didn't fully comprehend that there is a big difference from 'the Voice' that Lazarus heard internally and the appearance of an angel that would speak to him. You know me John, and you know that I am well aware of exactly what Lazarus meant by the manifestation of a voice being a disembodied presence that resonates within one's own mind, but you know full well that it isn't your voice. That is hard to explain to anyone that has never experienced such a manifestation, but Lazarus tried to describe it as best he could. So, the attempt by an editor trying to explain it as an angel was the best way for them to deal with a subject matter they couldn't fully comprehend. You can't explain what you don't understand, but as a Christian editor, whomever did make these edits, did have a very strong belief in angels."

"Wouldn't John have had a belief in angels as well?"

"Yes and no."

That answer only served to confuse Pearce even more. "Well, which is it?"

"At that time, angels were viewed as messengers to those that God did not have a direct relationship with. If the Lord had something important to say to someone, he would talk directly to that person. Prophecies usually required God's direct attention. High priests and members of the royal family had a direct line to the Almighty. The same was true for the major prophets. Samuel, Isaiah, Jeremiah, Ezekiel, Hosea, Joel,

Amos, Obadiah, Jonah, Micah, Nahum, Habakkuk, Zephaniah, Haggai, Zechariah, and even Malachi. It's not until you read Daniel that you find there is a different means of communication and that is through dreams. As you could see historically, if God wanted your attention he would speak to you directly without any middleman, If Jochanan or Lazarus wanted to be viewed as a major prophet, then he too would have written in a manner that showed he was spoken to directly."

"If that's the case…" I could see the wheels turning behind Pearce's eyes as he digested that God spoke to his prophets directly if he had an important message, "then why would an editor not retain that same format?"

"Let me see how I can answer that one for you," I had to think about the best way for me to deliver my answer without sounding offensive. "You have Jesus up on the cross saying, *'Eli, Eli, Lamah Sabatachni'* and getting no answer."

"My Father, My Father, why has thou forsaken me?"

"Not quite," I corrected him. "It's actually My God, My God. A common mistake perpetuated by the Church. But that's not my point. My point is that not even Jesus appears to have a direct line to God at that moment, so how is it that a much lesser person like this Jochanan or Lazarus could have one? Apparently, the editor or editors couldn't tolerate such an oversight by God , having Lazarus elevated to a position that would appear to be more sanctified than Jesus, so they introduce an angel so that they've now created a distance between God and his prophet. John is only worthy of receiving God's word as second-hand information."

"Like a buffer."

"Exactly."

Pearce swallowed hard. "You're suggesting they did it because otherwise Jochanan would be seen as being more significant than Jesus."

"You tell me. Jesus is long dead. He said he would return but he didn't. They said he died to absolve the world of sin, but in fact the world was sinning even more than ever. And whereas Jesus didn't spout with any details of a long-term prophecy, here was someone that was subservient to Jesus, an underling, doing exactly that. Lazarus seemed to know more about what was going to happen than Jesus did. There was no way the Church was going to tolerate that! It would defeat the entire concept that after Jesus there would be no more prophets required."

"It's complicated," Pearce attempted to obfuscate the obvious. Maybe it's a typical response when one finds their belief system challenged.

"Truthfully, it doesn't even appear to me as if these unidentified editors were even attempting to conceal their role in making glaring alterations right from the first sentence. They write that Jesus sent an Angel to his servant Jochanan, but it's a third person observation, rather than what one should have expected Lazarus to write, which would have been, *'And an angel appeared to me from Jesus.'* Then at least you would know that particular sentence comes directly from the mouth of Lazarus and not someone else."

"I presume you've got more instances than just that one," Pearce said somewhat snidely.

"Of course I do, but we will get to all of them in good time. The point I'm trying to make is that once all the third person edits are removed, along with the obvious unrelated Christian hyperbole, plus the attempts to divide the books as if it were distinct and separate letters being written to the various Christian Churches and enclaves, then what is left is naturally not only a much smaller composition, but it is only seven chapters in length and not the twenty-two that the document purports to contain. This is important because the number seven plays a big part in Jewish traditions, and this would have been well known by Lazarus. What remains following this literary surgical excision is a very Jewish prophetic book in its content but more importantly, one which in extremely ominous for our present times. It would appear that we are now standing at that precipice and unless we can act quickly to counter current events, then we have absolutely no way to escape the prophecy."

"Not sure if I'm following you Doc. Are you saying we have to throw away two thirds of the book because you consider fifteen of the twenty-two chapters to be falsifications?"

I shook my head. "No, I'm not saying that at all. What I am saying is that someone restructured and divided the original content of the book into fifteen additional segments because in their opinion they thought it would help the reader grasp what they considered important in sending a Christian related message. Each chapter would highlight a specific event, though not everything was sequential. Many of the described events were concurrent and therefore the separation into chapters actually weakens the overall impact that was originally intended and ultimately distorts the original message by fragmenting it."

"Now you're suggesting that they practically rewrote the entire story?" Pearce tried to make it sound like I was proposing some delusional conspiracy theory.

"Come on, John, you more than anyone would know how easy it is to distort a story through intentional editing. You work for the publishing industry. I'm certain you know every trick there is. In fact, the media of today has distorted almost every story being told so much that no one has faith in the media any longer."

"That's not the same thing Doc. Any editor will tell you that the main focus of any editing is to improve the flow of the story being told while still ensuring the plot line retains its integrity."

"In other words, you can significantly alter what was written to meet your desired outcome. Thank you for agreeing with me John."

"Wait a minute," Pearce objected. "That's not what I said."

"No, but it does imply the feasibility of exactly what I'm telling you. Let me provide you with an example. Working from the original Aramaic text and having removed the extraneous and obviously added Christian messages identified through the third-party references, then what remains of Chapter 1 is quite revealing in its content. When this is done, Lazarus admits to hearing, *I am The Aleph and The Tau, says The Lord, Yahweh, our God, He who was there at the beginning and will be at the end, The Almighty and there is no other.* That introduction in itself should tell you that it was not originally a Christian doctrine. Lazarus is emphasizing both the oneness and uniqueness of God. Notice that he emphasizes God's presence from the beginning to the end of time. There is no implication that somewhere in the middle of the timestream God decided to take human form and walk upon the earth. He didn't need to because he is omnipresent. The tenth sentence displays an obvious editorial liberty from a much later period because it refers to his being in the spirit of the Lord's Day. Do you know why that is an obvious insertion John?"

"Not really," he replied. "Seems okay to me. He's obviously seeing and hearing this calling on a Sunday. What could be possibly wrong with that?"

"Except that the Lord's Day on a Sunday as distinct from the Jewish Sabbath on Saturday was a concept that wasn't introduced into Christianity until Constantine's reforms over two hundred years later. So, what Lazarus really wrote was that he was engaged in his Sabbath prayers when he heard a voice and thought it must be coming from behind him. Does that sound familiar to you?"

"Sort of what you told me when we first met," Pearce recollected the statement I had made to him almost thirty years earlier.

"Just like I described it to you. That voice that said '*Kahana Koom*' and I looked all around trying to identify where it was coming from, not realizing that the source was within my own mind. But eventually I saw a staircase in my apparition whereas Lazarus describes his seeing seven of the seven branched menorahs, made of gold. *'And in the midst of seven golden menorahs was the likeness of a man, and this man wore the ephod and he was girded around his chest with a golden wrap. His head and his hair were like wool and as white as snow, while his eyes burned with fire. His feet were sturdy and strong like the brass of Lebanon but his voice was soft and flowed like the sound of rippling waters. In his right hand he held seven stars, and his other hand grasped a sharp lance. I could see that strength radiated from him like the Sun.'* Would you agree that is an apt description of what he said he saw."

Pearce nodded his head. "It sounds about right."

"Who do you think he was describing, John?"

"That's easy," Pearce responded. "It had to be Jesus."

"Or so you've been told," I challenged his assertion.

"Who else could it have been?"

"Now that is the question you should have asked your teacher while you were sitting in your classroom at Catholic school. Do you not think that Lazarus would have recognized Jesus if he had seen him, even if it was supposed to be an older version of him? Do you not think that the first thing he would have written in this book of Revelation was that he beheld Jesus in this vision. He doesn't say anything of that nature. Instead, he describes what appears to be an elderly High Priest, wearing the ephod of the priesthood and surrounded by seven menorahs that are similar to the one that stood in the Temple of Jerusalem."

"Seven menorahs because of the seven Eastern churches,' Pearce practically shouted.

"Is that your attempt to prove that it must have been Jesus that he saw? Exactly how many menorahs do you recall in your Church that last time you attended Mass, John?"

"There isn't one," he answered sheepishly.

"Exactly! There isn't one because in most Christian contexts the menorah is not a standard liturgical item. It is and always has been a universally recognized symbol of Judaism."

"Why do you think he saw seven menorahs?"

"I'm glad you asked that question. As I said before, the number seven holds profound significance in Judaism, representing completeness, holiness, and divine order. So it is not by accident that there happen to be seven of the seven branched menorahs. One of those menorahs represents the creation, where God created the world in six days and rested on the seventh, making it holy. That being the case then the second menorah represents that seventh day or the Sabbath, a day of rest and sanctity, observed every seven days. Observing Shabbat every seventh day is one of the most fundamental commandments God has given us. The third menorah represents the Shmita year, another commandment where every seventh year is considered a sabbatical year in which the land is allowed to rest, and debts are forgiven. The fourth represents the Jubilee year, which requires that following seven cycles of seven years, then that fiftieth year is to be considered a time to celebrate, a time of liberation and a time for land restoration. The fifth menorah is symbolic of a middle stage in life in which God has blessed us with the union of man and woman in the wedding ceremony during which there are seven blessings. The sixth menorah is lit when a man coms to the end of his life and family and friends will sit the seven days of mourning for the passing of a loved one. But the last or seventh menorah, that represents the gifts that God has bestowed on mankind. As written in Isaiah 11:2-3, these are wisdom, understanding, counsel, fortitude, knowledge, piety and the fear of breaking God's moral code. Together, these seven menorahs signify the completeness or perfection, the fullness of time and life cycles that God has given us and through our own foolishness, we are about to lose it all. Can you appreciate now why this imagery had nothing to do with the seven early Churches and everything to do with the existing philosophy of the seven menorahs that is a recognized principle of Judaism. Lazarus was confirming the authenticity of this Judaic principle. It has nothing to do with the so-called seven churches.'"

"If that wasn't Jesus that he saw, then who was it?" I knew that question would be coming next.

"First, you do agree that Jochanan doesn't recognize this man at all. It's not like he yells out, 'Hey Jesus, it's so good to see you again.' In fact, he doesn't have a clue as to the man's identity."

"Is that a question?" Pearce appeared to be avoiding giving me an answer.

"Yes that was a question," I confirmed. "So, yes or no? He doesn't' recognize this person."

Reluctantly he finally answered 'yes'. "So, who do you say it is?"

"I see the image and to me it is obvious that the man is a high priest, because he wears no crown. That immediately eliminates him as the Messiah. I know your Catholic teaching describes Jesus as both priest and member of the royal Davidic dynasty. So, you would think that if he's wearing the ephod and golden girdle of the High Priest, then he'd also be wearing something that was representative of kingship as well. But he isn't. There is no crown. That alone should have told you that the man he saw was not Jesus. Unlike any High Priest that we would think of, this man that he saw is carrying a weapon in his left hand and his legs are strong and sturdy suggesting a warrior. Except for one. There's only one man that could fit this description and that is Samuel."

"How do you figure it is Samuel," Pearce was surprised by my answer.

"Because Samuel was far more than just a high priest. He was also a judge and a prophet, which is even more astounding than the fact that a non-Aaronite was able to serve as a high priest. This makes him exceptional. Unlike any other priest, Samuel did wield a weapon and used it to kill as described in his books. Who other than the man that anointed both Saul and David as Kings of Israel would you expect to deliver a prophecy concerning the restorations of the Temple and the monarchy? That was his role and purpose in life. Why would he be any different in the afterlife? The physical description also matches that which we know of him. Only one man would have been appointed to herald the emergence of a new world order and that would be Samuel."

"I still don't see why it had to be Samuel," Pearce fiercely defended his belief that it was Jesus.

"Because of what we were told in Samual 2:35," I responded calmly. "Can I be any more specific than that?"

"Do you expect me to know what was written there," Pearce sounded irritated. "I many know a lot of the New Testament off by heart but the Old Testament is not a challenge I'm about to take."

"Let me refresh your memory. *'And I will raise Me up a faithful priest, that shall do according to that which is in My heart and in My mind; and I will build him a sure house; and he shall walk before Mine anointed forever.'* If we just pay attention to that last line, it tells you that Samuel will herald the coming of each messiah or anointed for an eternity. That would suggest even after his own death. Without Samuel, there could be no arrival of God's chosen redeemer.   Bottom line is without the appearance of Samuel, then an end of days prophecy isn't possible. Now you know what's written there. Try not to forget it."

Pearce was still struggling to digest my explanation. "If it's not about the seven churches, then how do you explain the seven stars he held in his other hand?"

"That's the easy part," I laughed, "now that I've made you aware of Samuel's role. The seven stars are the seven messianic periods of restoration."

"The what…?"

"Listen, I just told you that Samuel was appointed by God to essentially be the official anointer of each messiah. And every messiah is heralded through a conjunction of the planets, referred to as the messianic star, or what you'd be more familiar with

John as the Star of Bethlehem. There were believed to be seven planets at that time, so the number of possible alignments of four or more planets you would think would be quite high but that's not the case. The conjunctions are separated by hundreds of years. As such, the seven stars are the conjunctions that have occurred and those that will occur in the future. Each conjunction represents a messianic event. The exodus from Egypt, the conquest of Canaan, the formation and rule of Israel under the judges, the time of Kings, the restoration under Zerubbabel and Nehemiah, and the liberation by the Hasmoneans. These are all occasions where a savior has arisen to save the Children of Israel."

"That's only six Doc. Are you suggesting that Jesus was the seventh star? After all, just as you said, his birth was heralded by the Star of Bethlehem."

"The six I just provided all had to do with the creation, rise, restoration and liberation of Israel," I pointed out. "That's the common theme and it is always centered about Israel being restored, not about the actual deliverer. That last star at the time of Jesus was obviously about the regaining of freedom from Rome and the rebuilding of the nation."

"But Israel didn't regain its freedom at that time. In fact, it was practically annihilated by Rome," Pearce felt compelled to remind me of the history that I was already well versed with.

"And that's why this prophecy was delivered to Lazarus, suggesting that at some time in the future that seventh messianic event would occur, I told you that he and Jesus were about the same age. I'm betting that he was born under that star as well. Israel will be reborn, and a new Jerusalem will rise and be glorified. He was shown what would happen and was commanded to deliver that message to the world. He just didn't know when that would happen."

"Israel has been restored," Pearce was quick to point out. "I know you weren't around for the big announcement in 1948, so you may have missed it."

Pearce felt my icy glare bore through his chest. "Is that supposedly an attempt at sarcasm John, or is it humor? Don't take comedy up as a career because you're not very good at it. Now, are you here to listen or are you going to continually balk at everything I'm telling you?"

"I'm listening Doc. Really, I am."

"I'll forgive you then, because I'm positive you were confused by the next line in Revelation in which Lazarus wrote, '*And when I saw him, I fell at his feet like a dead man, and he laid his right hand upon me saying, Do not be afraid, for I am the eternity of the messiahs both priests and kings, those that have lived and died, and behold, I am alive to the eternity of eternities, amen, and I have the key of Death and of Sheol*' To someone raised as a Christian, I can see how you would think it was a reference to Jesus but if you were equally well versed in the Tanach, you'd know that in the book of Zechariah, he refers to there being two messiahs at the end of time. First comes the messiah of Aaron and then he is followed by the messiah of David. Hence the reference to both priests and kings and they would share in the anointment by Samuel."

"I still don't understand why Samuel."

"Simple answer is that Samuel served as I said as priest, prophet and lawgiver. In terms of his relationship with the people and with God, he was even greater than Moses or any of the patriarchs. His authority was unique and outside of the expected norm as established by the laws given to Moses. I guess most sermon givers don't spend a lot of time to explore the uniqueness of Samuel. He defies the law, he possesses rare gifts that exceed human ability, and he is provided a power and authority over a nation that exceeded that of kings. Why Samuel? Because of all that and much more. He holds the key to both Death and Sheol."

"What is Sheol?"

"It's the key to the entire origin of this prophecy," I responded.

"No, Doc, really, what is it?" Pearce was not about to accept my short, distinct answer.

"You want the technical answer, then here it is. Sheol is a term found in the Hebrew Bible that refers to the abode of the dead, a shadowy and indistinct realm where all souls, regardless of their moral conduct in life, are believed to descend after death. Unlike your Christian notions of Heaven and Hell, Sheol is not a place of reward or punishment. It is a neutral, subterranean domain where the dead reside in a state of quiet existence, often described as akin to sleep or unconsciousness. The concept is completely the antithesis of Christian beliefs. The inclusion of that one word in this prophecy tells you immediately that they were discussing Hebrew doctrine and therefore the origins of Revelation were Jewish. No doubt about it."

"You certain it isn't heaven, Doc. I'm not familiar with the term," Pearce struggled with the fact that the man in the prophecy wasn't holding the Keys to Heaven as would be the case with Jesus."

"Sheol is mentioned in books such as Genesis, Job, Psalms, and Ecclesiastes. In these texts, Sheol is portrayed as a dark and silent place, often associated with imagery of dust and forgetfulness. In Psalm 88:3–6, the psalmist laments, 'My soul is full of troubles, and my life draws near to Sheol. I am counted among those who go down to the Pit; I am a man who has no strength.' That certainly isn't heaven, John. Sheol is not reserved for the wicked alone. The righteous, too, enter Sheol upon death. It totally reflects the ancient Israelite worldview that death was a great equalizer, cutting across social and moral boundaries, a concept that Samuel was very familiar with but lost on Christians.

"Is this like purgatory?" Pearce was still attempting to grasp the concept.

"Only if you were a post-Persian exile Jew. When they came back from Persia, those Jews had been impacted by the foreign culture and their Jewish eschatological beliefs expanded to include concepts of resurrection and judgment. That's why we find in Daniel 12:2 the introduction of the notion of a final judgment, where the righteous would be raised to eternal life, and the wicked to everlasting contempt. For that to happen, Sheol had to become a temporary abode, awaiting divine judgment and resurrection, sort of like your purgatory. But the being talking to Lazarus obviously predates that much later belief and for him the only option after death is Sheol. Hence, it could only be Samuel."

"So, you're saying this was an early belief, but not the belief at the time of Jochanan. Correct?"

"Exactly. Now ask yourself why would Lazarus have a vison in which he is provided a glimpse into the ancient Israelite understanding of death as a shared human destiny. It's a completely non-Christian view of the afterlife. As I told you John, this book was originally Jewish Apocrypha and this man with the stars is Samuel. You're just going to have to accept that."

CHAPTER FIVE: DECEPTION

"If you examine chapter two carefully as it's written in your King James version, John, you will realize that it practically condemns the rise of Christianity and blames Lazarus for being part of that deception. That should be the point where most people should recognize the Jewish nature of the book if I haven't convinced you thus far. I find it almost strange that anyone could read this section and not come to that conclusion. How it is even possible to preserve the notion that Jochanan or Lazarus was acting through Christian inspired doctrine to me is unfathomable."

"I've read the book several times Doc, and I sure don't see it that way," Pearce protested.

"That's because you didn't want to see what was actually written. If your brain is focused on a particular point of view, then it is only human nature to fill in any gaps and pitfalls that would support your beliefs. We all do it. We may be having a bad day due to it being cold and rainy, while feeling miserable over something in our lives, but later if the sun comes out and we see a rainbow, then we try to convince ourselves that it is a sign that everything is going to get better soon. We see what we wish to believe the same way that we believe what we wish to see."

"Well, who's to say that's not what you did when you read this chapter," Pearce challenged my interpretation.

Except that my interpretation is based on what is actually written. When Samuel says to Lazarus, '*I know your works, your toil and your patience, and that you cannot tolerate the evil ones, and you have tested those who claim to be Apostles, and they are not, and you have found them false,*' it is clear that he is referring to a specific people that Lazarus has separated himself from and has recognized that they were evil and now he wants nothing to do with them. Superficially, it would appear that it is a condemnation of those within the Minean or Christian community that speak out against Lazarus and therefore those are the ones to be considered as false apostles. But exactly who he is referring to is answered in the following sentences. '*But I have something against you, because you have left your former love.*' There can be no doubt about it, Lazarus is being accused of having turned his back on God for a period of time. The former love is a reference to his abandonment of his original Jewish faith. As God is the lover to the Children of Israel, and Israel is His bride as defined in much of the Tanach, then Lazarus betrayed this love by promoting Christian beliefs for a period of time. In that case, the evil ones are not apostles that preach a false narrative of Jesus, but all of Jesus's apostles as Samuel is calling out their preaching as being false. This is further emphasized in sentence five when Samuel tells him, '*Remember from where you have come out and do the former works; but if not, I will come against you and I will remove your menorah, unless you repent.*' Very strange if you still consider it a Christian work, as then he would have been encouraged to embrace his later devotion of faith to a new religion rather than his former one which was Judaism. In other words, what Samuel is saying is, 'Remember who you were, remember you were a faithful and practicing Jew, a true heir to the throne and the bearer of the seventh menorah that heralds the rebirth and restoration of the nation. But if you don't, you're going to experience the wrath of God."

"You're saying that in his later life, John was willing to abandon his faith in Jesus," Pearce's mind was attempting to paraphrase what I was telling him.

"First of all, let's not refer to him as John. If you want to hold on to calling him Jochanan, then do so but it would be best if you acknowledge him as Lazarus at this point and then it will make it easier to understand everything else, I'm going to explain to you. And secondly, Samuel is pretty clear on this not being a case of abandoning his beliefs in Jesus, it has to be a total rejection of anything the other apostles had to say. I don't think the statement that he can no longer tolerate the evil and falsehoods of these apostles can be interpreted in any other way then absolute rejection."

"But there were false apostles that never knew Jesus and were spreading false stories. Perhaps he was only referring to those," Pearce still attempted to defend his long-standing beliefs.

"Except when you examine sentence six when Samuel says, *'That you hate the works of the Naqolaytans.'* The funny thing about that is that there were never a people or a place that existed that was referred to as Nicolatia."

Pearce objected, "Sure there was. They were this sect of Christianity that preached a false religion. They were called the Nicolatians."

"Undocumented, without any other reference in Christian histories but only mentioned in this book, Revelation. Don't you think that is a bit suspicious. If I was to tell you, as well as insist that a cult of blood-sucking unicorn worshippers existed in Montreal, but no one else had ever seen them and there were no reports to be found that supported their existence, would you believe me or not?"

"Of course not," Pearce rejected my ridiculous assertion.

"And why not?" I pressed him on the matter. "If you know me to be an honest person and I swear to you that they do exist, then why would you doubt me?"

"Because everyone knows there are no such things as blood-sucking unicorns."

"Only because you haven't seen one yourself but that's not a reason why you should doubt my word."

"Doc, I'd probably suggest you stay off the booze."

"Considering no one else has ever reported seeing one or has provided any evidence of their existence, you can probably assume it was just a figment of my wild imagination. But why in the world would theologians come to the conclusion that there must be a sect called Nicolatians based on the singular mention of the word by a man about to have visions of the end of the world and there being no other reference anywhere else of such a cult?"

"What else could it possibly mean, if he wasn't referring to a group of false believers?"

"I'm glad you asked that question, John. It was one that should have been asked a long time ago, but I suspect members of the clergy did everything possible to ensure it was never asked, so that they would not have to find the correct answer."

"And I presume you are going to tell me now that you have the answer," Pearce has been around me long enough to know that I wouldn't raise a scenario unless I had a purpose.

"Am I that obvious? I guess so," I answered my own question. "Naqolaytan is an Aramaic word that translates as 'The Fraudulent Ones', That's why you had the belief that there was a particular people call Nicolatians that practiced a false Chrisitan religion. But it is not a noun but an adjective. The fact that Lazarus had come to detest this collective of people spreading a false religion, and that Samuel says, *'Those things which I also hate,'* it would suggest that these teachings are both prominent and widespread, thereby coming to the attention of God, Himself. It's not some small and insignificant sect that he is referring to, but instead the totality of all the groups that preached Christian doctrine at that time. Those spreading Christianity, any Christianity, are identified as his enemies or the fraudulent ones. Do you see it now?"

"Sort of," was all that Pearce had to say.

"Then you'll enjoy this next part from sentence seven. *'He who has an ear to hear, let him hear what the spirit is speaking to these assemblies, and I shall give to the victor to eat of the tree of life, which is in the Paradise of God.'* It's the opposite of what you are probably thinking. He was being told to listen to what was actually being said in the Christian assemblies and by resisting their message, to become the victor, and God would reward him for it. As for the spirit, he's not talking about the Holy Spirit as you may have been taught to believe. A spirit can be righteous or malevolent and in this case the suggestion is that a mischievous and dishonest spirit is speaking and leading the assemblies astray."

"What makes you think the spirit is evil?" Pearce questioned.

"Because he indicates that there is a struggle taking place, and only if one listens closely to what the spirit is saying and recognizes if for being false, will they become victorious and be welcomed by God. Why do you think a word like victor was used if there wasn't an opposing force to be victorious over?"

"That still doesn't prove the spirit is preaching a falsehood," he insisted.

"It does when you look at what is written in sentence nine, *'and the blasphemy of those who call themselves Jews of the Judeans, when they are not, but are the synagogue of Satan.'* If the Jews are the actual Judeans, then those that are calling themselves by that title must be a group proclaiming themselves to be Jews but obviously believing in something very different from mainstream Judaism. They are a counter force to Judaism, and in fact, they are referred to as being a Church of Satan. At that time, the only group of Jews, that were proclaiming themselves to be the real Jews but practicing a faith that was confrontational to the concept of Jewish monotheism were the Mineans. That is the Church that is being referred to and it is poignant that these Mineans didn't refer to their congregation as a Church but as a synagogue. That is the evil being identified. The only threat to the survival of Judaism were those Jews that insisted they were Jewish but practiced something completely different. Only when you call them out for it will you be victorious. The writing is pretty clear if you really want to understand it," I advised.

"You're saying I am intentionally trying not to accept what you are telling me," Pearce attempted to make it sound like an accusation.

"Yes, I am. It is crystal clear what was written but for two thousand years, Christian theologians have tried to obfuscate and disguise the obvious."

"Maybe it's not as obvious as you think it is," Pearce suggested.

"Only if you don't understand the definition of blasphemy," I countered. "You do know what that word means, right John? A blasphemer is someone that disrespects God or that which is holy. The Jews, or should I say the real Jews living in the diaspora and Judea, were essentially practicing in the same manner that had been explained and taught to them by Moses, fourteen hundred years earlier. That being the case, they couldn't be the ones accused of blaspheming. But Jews that suddenly wanted to turn the entire faith upside down, altering monotheism into polytheism, essentially creating a demigod that took the indescribable and adorned him with human flesh, now that would undoubtedly be blasphemy. And that is exactly what the Mineans did. Perhaps not exactly a synagogue of Satan, because I'm certain their motivation wasn't purely for the sake of doing evil, but in the eyes of a true believer, they might as well have been Satan, himself."

Pearce paused, his mind beginning to absorb that which I was explaining. I could see that my last statement had left him momentarily speechless. It was logical and it was concise, and those are the arguments that can dull anyone's claws.

"You're not going to let me keep my beliefs in peace," Pearce knew he was in trouble, "Are you?"

"Don't you want to hear the rest I have to say?" I think I may have started feeling a little sorry for him, but not that sorry. "I can stop if you want me to, but that doesn't mean I'm not going to publish the book. It's either going to be through your publishing house or someone else."

Pearce sighed. "I've gone down the road with you this far, so, I might as well go all the way. After all, you still need someone to critique this story."

"Well then, let's move on to sentence fourteen because it is equally revealing. *'But I have a few things against you, for you have there, those who hold the doctrine of the Balaam,'* I'm certain that one threw a few curveballs at a lot of priests and ministers. In case you don't remember Balaam had the gift of prophecy but instead of using his gift to help the Jewish population in Canaan, he used it instead to aid the Moabite king. The point there is that this man was given a gift of divination from the God of the Jews but decided to use it against the Jews. As my grandmother would say, 'that took a lot of chutzpah, after all, he was practically slapping God across the face. As a very prominent Jewish community leader, with the rare gift of prophecy, as this sentence would indicate existing long before he ever wrote Revelation, Lazarus was behaving exactly like Balaam. Lazarus threw his lot in with a group of fringe radicals that in many ways were preaching a false religion that held the potential to destroy the Jewish nation. Hence his comparison of Lazarus to Balaam and the Christians as a whole being nothing more than Balaq, the King of the Moabites. He is suggesting that Lazarus had been a disgrace before God, guilty of casting a stumbling block before the Children of Israel, causing many to go astray and begin eating the sacrifices of idols and committing fornication."

"Don't you think that accusation is a little extreme Doc. As if he made them actually sacrifice to idols and fornicate," Pearce attempted to laugh off my statement as hyperbole.

"Hey, I didn't say that. Go back and read revelation. That's what was written, and it is easy to understand why. Not only was the 'Son of God' a pagan concept, but the use of relics and charms smacked of idolatry. I can't speak to the early sexual practices of the Christian community, but obviously the sentence was a condemnation of their doing something that resembled the sacred prostitutes of the pagan temples. Guilt for the rise in popularity of Christianity is being laid directly at Lazarus's feet. There was only one way to rectify his mistakes and that is by repenting, as explained in sentence sixteen of this chapter. He has to do something that will bring back those that went astray, otherwise Samuel is threatening to destroy all of them. And as you know from the history of his own books, Samuel was not one to make idle threats. When it came to eradicating entire tribes of people, few in the Tanach can match Samuel for such zealousness."

"And that something you're suggesting was to write this book,"

"That's clear from sentence 19 where Samuel says, *'I know your works, your love, your faith, your service and your patience, and your latter works are more than the first.'* By later works, the terminology is referencing this book of Revelation. Suggesting it will have a far greater impact, in the shortest possible time. It will be his greatest writing and will rectify the damage done to Judaism by his former writings which glorified Jesus. Once again, you get a clear indication that Revelation was intended as a Hebrew prophetic manuscript," I suggested. "And what is written in the next sentence is about as descriptive a condemnation of Christianity that you will ever encounter. *'I have much against you, because you are tolerating your wife Jezebel who says about herself that she is a Prophetess and teaches and seduces my Servants to commit fornication and to eat the sacrifices of idols.'* Self-explanatory. What more needs to be said?"

It was a leading question but when it looked like Pearce was about to attempt to answer it, I knew I better cut him off quickly. "I know," I stated firmly. "I know what you're about to say. But your Christian scholars interpret it as a condemnation of a number of false preachers in Christianity that were leading the followers down a false path. And what false path could that possibly be?" I proclaimed. "That he was the son of Almighty God? That he was born of a virgin? That he was the messiah, although none of the final prophecies as provided by the elder prophets was ever fulfilled? So, tell me John, what could any of these false doctrines have stated that could be any more blasphemous to the movement's early Jewish roots. Take a good look at the simile or metaphor being used as the comparison, John. Jezebel was one of the most infamous figures reviled in the Old Testament, renown for her practice of idolatry, manipulation of her husband, King Ahab, and her opposition to the true prophets of God. If we comprehend Jezebel's marriage to Ahab as being more than a political alliance, but an actual compromise of the stringent Hebrew beliefs into a more easily tolerated religious system that resembled what was practiced by the rest of the world, then we can understand that in the same way, Christianity was intended to be a dilution of the monotheistic pillar erected in Israel, so that it could be appreciated and more easily coexist with the Roman pagan world. Lazarus is being condemned for participating in permitting Jews to be led astray from their core beliefs. Like Ahab, he may not have been the initiator of the crime, but he did nothing to try and stop Jezebel and therefore is guilty of aiding and abetting. The next couple of sentences are a forewarning to those that continue to follow the Christian path, that they will eventually have to pay for their failure to repent. The reference to children of these adulterers is simply an indication that it will be many generations before the actual punishment is meted out but sentence 26 provides an escape clause to those that return the original Jewish faith of their ancestors. In their cases, they will share in the restoration of the orderly Kingdom of God that will be revealed by Lazarus's prophecy. As Samuel states on behalf of the Lord, '*I know your works, and behold, I have set an open door before you which no man can shut, because you have a little power, and you have kept my word and have not denied my name.*' This is a recognition that those that continue to follow Judaism will become a minority within a world dominated by those that practice this false faith that Lazarus contributed to. God sees how little power they had in this vast sea of contempt and intolerance, hatred and prejudice, but still they never abandoned their Jewish faith, clinging to it despite incredible odds and for that reason he will never close the door to their salvation. Do you see what I'm telling you John?"

"I can't say that I agree with everything you said, Doc, but I won't deny that you may have a valid point or two."

"Well, I guess that's better than having no valid point at all," I laughed. "Having stripped away much of what appears to be later additions and references to assemblies that bore no connection to the subject matter of Judaism that was being discussed, I think by now it should be evident that the core concepts of this particular book are closely aligned with Jewish religious traditions."

"Is that everything you got Doc?" Pearce questioned me. "You removed any reference that he made of writing to the various churches which would have shown he was still actively promoting their teachings."

"Because as I said at the beginning of our discussion, they didn't belong there. They were much later additions provided to hide the actual message of what was being said. Remember, you're reading the King James version. I'm using a much older Aramaic version."

"But you stripped away half of the chapter in which it was clear that Jesus was talking to Jochanan and describing the events of the various churches."

"Yes, I did," I agreed. "I never said there wasn't a lot of additions made to the original manuscript by these Christian editors. Think of it as being an archeologist, John. One may need to remove a ton of rubble and dirt in order to find a single shard of bone that fits into the palm of your hand. That ton rubble may have its own story as to how it came to be lying there but none of it is as important as that miniscule fragment that was uncovered. Think of me as that archeologist and I'm finding these incredible artifacts that have been waiting two thousand years to be uncovered."

"But that which you refer to as rubble has tremendous value as well," Pearce insisted. "You can't just indiscriminately do away with it just because you believe it doesn't belong to the artifact you found."

"If it was meant to be attached, then by discarding it, that would mean that what was left would appear incomplete and unable to be viewed as coherent. Having only a part of the whole would fail to tell a complete story. There'd be too many gaps, too many holes that were so big, you'd be able to drive a car through them. But if what I reveal to you after stripping away all this other material that you believe is essential, and what I have still appears to be complete, rational, sensical and relevant story, then you must admit that there's a good possibility that I am correct in my original assertation."

"Then I don't think you provided enough information to draw that conclusion," Pearce challenged my hypothesis. "You finished your argument but there's so much more written regarding the churches that you were selectively picking from a limited amount of material to support your hypothesis."

"As I said John, I'm using an Aramaic text as my source for Revelation."

"Well, it must be wrong then. It has to be corrupted from the real text."

"What makes you think that, John?

"Think what?"

"That its corrupted?"

"Because it is missing so much. It's actually a much older version than the Greek translations used for the King James Version. Older should immediately tell you that it is more likely to be authentic."

"You haven't proven that yet."

'What makes you think I was finished with my argument. We've only dealt with the first two chapters of Revelation. There's still thirteen more to go. By the time I'm finished you are going to be very familiar with the Aramaic Peshitta." I could actually hear him sigh when I said that.

CHAPTER SIX: THE GOOD

"Are we finished our coffee break?" I questioned Pearce, "Because I'd like to get back to what we were discussing." It was obvious that Pearce was attempting to avoid any further discussion regarding the book of Revelation. "Why don't I recap for you quickly what we've already discussed so that we have the baseline set for what we'll discuss next."

Pearce reluctantly nodded his head.

"Samuel, as the spokesperson for Yahweh, both admonishes Eleazar for his abandonment of his inherited task or mission and for straying from the true faith, only to praise him for finding it again and resuming the mission that had been originally given to him. There obviously is still this unhappiness on the part of the Lord that so many had followed this new path that they were referring to as 'true Judaism' but from their interaction, it would appear that it was not expected to last much longer as they were discussing its eventual end, measured in generations. This coming storm would wash away the Mineans or early Christians but at the same time, it was probably this mistaken belief that the restoration would be soon, that encouraged the rabbis to select a messiah to lead them against Hadrian. But that's an entirely different story as you know from my book, **Beneath A Falling Star.** It was a foolish notion on their part, because Messiahs aren't selected by men; they are appointed by God, which is also the clear message being delivered in the first couple of chapters of Revelation. That essentially condenses what we have discussed thus far. Would you agree.?"

Rather than say anything, Pearce just continued to nod his head.

"You're not exactly happy with my take on this story," I prodded.

"Well, first of all, you're wrong," he seemed happier as he pointed his finger, "Christianity didn't die out after several generations as you were suggesting. In fact, it became stronger and is the largest denomination in the world presently."

"Actually, it did die out. Two hundred and twenty years or so, after Lazarus died, the Christianity that he was dealing with did come to an end. It took about five generations but this hybrid of Judaism and Messianic fanaticism did come to an abrupt end, only to be hijacked and replaced by something completely different, under the authority of politically appointed oligarchs, claiming divine authority and inspiration. I'm sorry John, but that's the truth. Constantine changed everything and without realizing it, that is the foundation subject matter that underscores the entire book of Revelation."

"What...I don't get it."

"You will as we get into more detail but for now, just keep in mind that without this tremendous upheaval, there would not be this eventual failure of mankind that results in a Doomsday scenario."

"You're suggesting the advent of Christianity is the reason God is threatening to bring about the end of days. That's absurd!" he shouted.

"Calm down, John. Let me explain it another way. When God gave the Torah or Law to Moses, it was with the express purpose that the Israelites would become the 'Or Ha-Oylum' or 'Light Unto the World.' You're well aware of that adage. But have you ever thought about what that actually meant as a gift to mankind?"

"Well…" Pearce began to answer but I cut him off immediately

"That was a rhetorical question, John. I'm going to answer it for you. The first deliverable, if I can call it that, was morality. God essentially was giving man a means by which to evaluate right from wrong. Mankind was out of control, and it needed a moral compass. But with that outline of morality comes freewill as God is saying this is what you should do but still permitting the individual to consciously make the choice of how they will behave."

"Which is where Satan comes in," John interjected. "Having free will also means you're subject to temptation."

"Don't try to introduce concepts that were never there in the first place," I cautioned him. "The devil is nothing more than an excuse, so a person doesn't have to accept the blame for their own decisions and behaviour. Evil doesn't exist."

"Sure, it does," he insisted.

"For something to actually exist, it must have its own distinct origin. As I just pointed out, 'the Good', does have such an origin. God gave us the Torah and it was a guideline on being good. Follow its instructions and you will be a good person. If man didn't know what the definition of good was before, he certainly knew it once instructions were provided by God. But at the same time, mankind became aware that if I don't follow these instructions, then I am not good. Therefore, that which we consider evil is merely the absence of doing what the Torah described as good. The absence of being good is essentially what we refer to as evil. As you can see, it doesn't have its own set of rules and only manifests when that which is good is rejected or not present. It is more a case of either being good or not good and by giving us free will, the decision as to which path we will follow has been left to us. We are the force that you commonly refer to as evil if we choose not to take the good path presented to us by God."

"That would mean that Satan already exists within us," Pearce somehow extrapolated this moral absence I was referring to and transformed it into and actual presence of the devil. "That's why it's referred to as original sin."

"No, that's not what I said. If you had listened to me, then you would have grasped the essential take away point, which was that if you use your freewill to reject God's words, then you will be subject to moral decay and that is what you wish to refer to as Satan, but which is actually the innate characteristic of all living creatures. When survival is threatened every animal, especially humans will revert to their most primitive instincts, but in the case of humans, that include murder, rape, infanticide, thievery, dishonesty and every other conceivable evil you can imagine. That's the level from which mankind raised itself up from once God provided us with his commandments and showed us what was right. But if and when we choose to reject the 'Good' that He has given us, then we revert to that base level and recreate the evil. It has always been our choice, but it is so much easier to accept our savage nature if we can blame it on something else such as a devil that seduces us with temptation and makes us perform those evil deeds."

"I disagree," Pearce objected to my reasoning of good versus evil. "Mankind doesn't want to sin. That's why we embrace Jesus into our lives but there are those that work for Satan and they have no other purpose but to confuse us and make us sin. Jesus died to absolve us of our sins and because of that, Satan is determined to bring us back to original sin."

"So, how's that working for you?"

"What do you mean?"

"Just what you said. Jesus died to absolve you of your sins but Satan just keeps dragging you back in…John, it was not my intention to engage you in some theological discussion regarding original sin but when you start spouting crap I have no other choice. The fundamental truth of humanity is that when left to our own devices, we willingly do that which is wrong and if so, then we are Satan. The devil doesn't exist because we all have the potential to perform evil deeds naturally, and when we do, every one of us becomes the devil incarnate."

"That's not true," he protested. "Human nature is naturally swayed to do good but it is difficult because we are constantly being led astray. But you want me to believe that we are at that threshold of constantly becoming our own devils. That mankind in general prefers to do evil. That's what you're suggesting," Pearce began raising his blood pressure as could be seen by his face turning a shade of scarlet.

"Not at the threshold," I shook my head. "I believe we have crossed it and that is why I raised the issue of our primeval survival instincts. All creatures are driven by what I call the three 'S' laws of existence, sex, sustenance and sleep. Deprive us of any one of those and we will do whatever it takes in order to obtain them, even commit murder."

Pearce dismissed my statement with a wave of his hand. "That's ridiculous!"

"You think so," I challenged him. "The pursuit of sex beyond the traditional norms as outlined in the bible have resulted in a surge of sex crimes that exceed the levels of any other civilizations over the record of mankind. The rapes, the drugging of women, the kidnapping of children and young girls to recruit into the sex-slave market, the level of adultery, sodomy, and sexual violence within our societies, they are all skyrocketing. Are you even aware that one in five women will be raped at sometime during their lives. That is a horrifying number. It should terrify you if you have daughters. And if a twenty percent rape indicator isn't enough to convince you, then did you know that forty-three percent of heterosexual women, forty-six percent of lesbians and seventy-five percent of bisexual woman will be victims of sexual violence. It is freewill that makes all that possible, but it is the moral decay of society that permits it to continue. A God-fearing, righteous and morally upstanding society would put an end to it. But governments, educational systems, even those that consider themselves to be the intellectually elite all disparage the belief in God and undermine the fundamental beliefs as laid out in the bible. It's time you start asking yourself, 'Why are they so eager to do that? Why are they so determined to stop others from believing in God?' This is not a conspiracy theory as there is always an underlying reason for those in power failing to confront these issues head on, while at the same time attempting to convince you that this is all normal and don't worry about it because they have it safely under control. You need to ask yourself what does safely under control actually mean when there's a good chance one of your daughters is going to be raped."

Pearce was finally paying attention to what I was saying. "But they don't have it under control," he agreed. "I'm not stupid, I know that. They just tell us that to try and keep us calm and from becoming overly distraught."

"What's wrong with becoming emotional and distraught?" I pressed him. "Why shouldn't we demand they put an end to it immediately? Why not castrate every sex offender we manage to catch?"

Pearce was lost for an answer. Finally, he spoke up, "They can't get it under control."

"Depends on how you define control," I snapped back. "Every year there are close to 325,000 children abducted into child sex and labour trafficking around the world. The American government will say that they have it under control because only around 13 of those children enter into the United States daily. Sounds okay when you present it that way, until you start doing the math and realize that amounts to 4,745 children a year. And that's based only on an estimate from reports they receive and children that have been rescued What about all the ones they don't know about?. More likely that it is three or four times that amount. That would mean over 5% of all the children taken worldwide end up in the United States. Now ask yourself, how many tens of thousands of Americans are abusing those children once they arrive? You don't actually think it is one abducted child for a single pedophile, do you? Of course not! There'd be no money for a business that was marketing to a single buyer to survive for very long. More like ten, twenty, perhaps even a hundred customers per child. How many millions of dollars are being spent by those with power and money to abuse these children. And that is when you realize what being under control means. When the same people that hold the reins of power are either rubbing elbows or are actively participating with those involved in such perverse and evil behavior, and being rewarded for it, why would they try to put an end to it? Let's be honest about it. The perpetuation of such evil lies within the domain of the filthy rich and powerful. That being the case, then control really means keeping the public unaware of the full extent of the truth. That's why nothing has been released about the Epstein murder because then they would have to provide the list of all those that wanted to see him dead because they feared being exposed. As I told you, we are definitely at that threshold, but the information is certainly not being made available for 'we' the people to be aware of the precariousness of the situation."

"What about the sustenance and sleep that you mentioned as also being key components forcing people to turn to evil?" Pearce sill wanted more information before accepting my reasoning.

"Our sexual perversions aren't enough to convince you that we are the devil incarnate?" I questioned somewhat mockingly. "Sustenance implies you have enough food and material objects to provide for stable life. That is the enigma of our times. We are probably the richest in terms of personal assets that mankind has ever been over its history, but what we consider to be our basic requirements for sustaining life has been inflated and exaggerated to the point of desiring everything. It's not merely about food on the table in order to survive. Instead, the food has to come from either fast-food chains or Michelan level restaurants, only to be washed down with expensive liquor or gold label wines. Clothes are no longer designed to simply keep us warm but now must display the signature of a top designer on the label. It is no longer about what is essential or practical anymore because it is all about preserving status. But status requires money, a commodity that is restricted to a minority of people, so many from the majority are driven towards crime in order to obtain it. The sad fact is that what was once an evil committed by those that were desperate and driven by survival, has become an equal opportunity activity for the spoiled, even more than the needy. That's why you have laws like the one that they established in California that you can shoplift goods without any penalty as long as you don't exceed a thousand dollars. That only encourages further criminal behavior and feeds the sickness of never having achieved a satisfactory balance of sustenance. Society is given a pass to break another commandment of God, Thou Shall Not Steal, and now there are many that embrace the right to commit a crime of theft openly.

As for sleep, in order to have a good night's sleep you require a roof over your head. There was a time that was practically a given for everyone. Families ensured everyone had a place to sleep, no matter what your status was in society. But what is being referred to as chronic homelessness is now at an all-time high and shows no indications of dissipating. Tent cities aren't a life choice, they're a choice of desperation and a sure sign of a decaying society. Squatting in homes that belong to someone else should surely be considered a crime, yet it is the homeowner that is often fined as the criminal party or held in contempt of court for trying to evict the squatters. In essence our legal system is willing to approve breaking the commandment not to covet their neighbour's belongings. Our failure to adhere to the laws handed down to Moses convinces me that we are at the precipice. And it's not even a matter of adhering to the Ten Commandments, but in reality it appears to be a deliberate attempt to negate them."

"Because the Devil is exploiting our weakness," Pearce insisted.

"Bull-shit, John. Keep trying to convince yourself it isn't a result of our own nature. I told you; man possesses all the qualities of the Devil and only by suppressing them through a sense of righteousness and moral obligation does he keep them in check. That is why this book has become so important at this particular point in time. We can't afford to let ourselves sink much lower than we already have. Either we turn the tide now and save what is left of our fragile world or everything that Lazarus described will come to fruition. Guaranteed!"

"But you still haven't told me why it is necessary for you to undermine the Christian heritage of the book and claim it as one of the Jewish apocrypha in order to achieve the goal of informing the public of our decline. The doomsday prophecies are just as relevant and important for every Christian as well that still believes in the Bible," he pleaded for me to not challenge its origins.

"I'm only doing so because I was instructed to review the book and reveal it as a Jewish manuscript."

"What's so important about it being something other than a Christian document?" Pearce demanded to know.

"As a Christian document, it is limited," I explained. "As I already told you, the development of Christianity was an unintentional mishap that resulted from those preaching its messages moving further and further away from the religion's Jewish heritage. That's clearly the message that Samuel is delivering to Lazarus. It's essential that it is restored to reaffirm that heritage."

"Why?" was all that Peace had to say.

"Because!" I was tempted to leave that as my one word answer to his repetitive asking of 'Why'. But I knew that wouldn't stop him. "With the introduction of Christian imagery, it has been made to look more like a fantasy movie, than an actual prophecy. Christianity is declining because in today's world of scientific facts and genetic knowledge, the insistence on the creation of a human being from anything other than two humans is unacceptable. The argument to dissuade anyone from following Christianity is too strong because of your emphasis on immaculate conception, which defies our own level of scientific knowledge regarding the procreation of life."

"That's the miracle," Pearce tried to explain.

"Except even miracles have to follow the fundamental laws of nature, and that requires an X and a Y chromosome, within a total of forty-six chromosomes resulting from a fertilized ovum."

"Well, why couldn't have God just doubled the chromosomes in one of Mary's eggs. That would still follow the natural law you're talking about."

"Because if that was the case, then Jesus would have been a woman and everyone would have remarked on how much she resembled her mother, almost as if she had been cloned as a twin. Which is exactly what she would have been. I have no issue with Jesus being a teacher, and someone that actually fulfilled the prophecies. I say as much in my book *The Caiaphas Letters*. But this Christian insistence on his having to be the son of God is the major deterrent as to why most of the world ignores the Book of Revelation."

"And that's why you think you're being instructed to restore it to original Judaic roots," Pearce surmised. "How's that going to change anyone's perspective?"

"Judaism's main feature is its moralistic and philosophical approach to life. It demands that you live your life as a good person more than you need to fulfil the rituals associated with a deity or in your case a trinity. Everyone that lives a good life will be rewarded, without having to fully some ritual dogma."

"But you have your rituals too," Pearce countered. "In fact, you have plenty of them."

"That's true but the decalogue doesn't insist on how you are to perform them. Look at the first four commandments. You are commanded to have no other gods. That means no pantheon, no sons, no daughters, not even demi-gods. All that's required is just to acknowledge the universe was the result of one supreme being and He is satisfied with you. You don't have to be Jewish to acknowledge that. The second prohibits idols, but what we don't seem to realize is that it includes Hollywood, political or artist idols as well. Today, we have reached a point in society where we hold these people in such high regard that they're actually being worshipped practically as gods. Not all idols are made out of stone and wood. Some are forged from flesh and bone. And practically no Christian understands what taking God's name in vain means. They think it refers to using it in the context of a swear word but in truth it is referring to swearing an oath to God while having no intention of fulfilling that oath or it is merely used as a ploy to magnify one's own vanity. By doing so, you are forcing God to punish you for your intentional deceit."

Peace scratched his head. "I'm having difficulty following that one."

"The story of Jephthah is the perfect example of that. As his oath, Jephthah swore he would sacrifice the very first thing that came out of his house to greet him as a sign of gratitude to the Lord for granting him victory over the Ammonites. A foolish oath as soon as it is analyzed because simply put, one does not keep their livestock in their house. Therefore, he was bragging that he would sacrifice something that he cherished because it was living within his home. Perhaps he was thinking of his dog or his cat, neither of which was a fitting sacrifice or perhaps he made the oath with no intention of needing to fulfill it at all following his victory. After all, he would be the great hero that defeated the Ammonites and everyone would be bowing down to him. Who could dare to insist that he had to fulfil that vow, since he had become master of them all?"

"But he did keep that vow?" Pearce recalled the story in Judges.

"Only upon realizing that once his daughter greeted him with dancing and music, then he knew God made her do that on purpose to teach him a lesson. He recognized that God would not let him break his oath without demanding a severe punishment. He became aware that he was bound to that oath and he became panicked."

"I've always hated that story," Pearce commented with a look of disgust on his face. "It never made any sense to me as to why God would have permitted him to sacrifice his daughter. It goes against the very concept of God being benevolent and loving. The girl was innocent. Since when does God demand the sacrifice of the innocent?"

"God doesn't but the story is there for a reason. God compromises on many things throughout the Old Testament and even lets himself be negotiated and hustled as we witness Abraham doing it repeatedly to Him, as in the story concerning Lot, but when it comes to disobeying the Ten Commandments, there has to be a penalty. It just may not have been what Jephthah was willing to offer."

"But to permit human sacrifice? That is already too much. God forbids human sacrifice! It crosses the line and goes against everything we believe about the nature of God."

"True," I admitted, "It seems harsh and is contrary to our belief at first glance of a loving and merciful god, but when you dig down deeper into the story, you will see a different perspective. Believe me when I say there was an escape clause, there was an out, but Jephthah didn't take it," I informed Pearce.

"What out? He was trapped by his own words," Pearce insisted. "God demanded he had to fulfil his vow."

"The key to the escape clause is buried in the third sentence of this chapter in Judges. Do you recall what that said?"

"Do you really expect me to remember everything in the Bible word for word," Pearce shrugged.

"Jephthah was Gilead's illegitimate son and as a result, he was not allowed to share in his father's inheritance, being driven out of the home by his stepbrothers, as we are told for a specific purpose. It's not random information, it is actually highly significant. Take notice, that at no other time does the bible refer to Gilead being anything other than a geographical location. Now, to have Gilead mentioned as a real person and the tribal founder of the Gileadites, which was not one of the original twelve tribes, then this is significant as it is informing you just how powerful and wealthy that family must have been to receive this recognition and have the land bear his name. Being rejected certainly was not a good start in life for Jephthah, but God felt mercy towards him and helped him to become a great warrior and a leader in his own right. We know that because as we are told in that third sentence, he had gathered a lot of admirers around him because of his mighty reputation. The vanity of these men, as it is described, is that they fought for Jephthah's glory and essentially worshipped his greatness over that of God's. Based on his reputation, the Gileadites offered to make Jephthah their ruler if he should win the battle for them. They're not praying to God for a victory, but instead decided on their own accord to raise up their own king and believed that would seal their victory."

"But it says he did pray to God to grant him victory."

"But not at first. We just read about Ahimelech, and now the people once again wish to raise a ruler over themselves, forgetting that God is King. Of course, Jephthah is more than happy to become their leader, but he only turns to God when he was unable to establish a peaceful resolution with the Ammonites through negotiations and suddenly there was no alternative but going to war. So, it is the intention of the story to make us realize that Jephthah being the vain-glorious, narcissistic man that he was, never appreciating that his success was only provided by the grace of God, saw himself as the center of the universe, and it is in that context that he made his oath to God. It was made without sincerity and without any forethought."

"So, where's this escape hatch you mentioned."

"His oath was that he specifically would perform the sacrifice but that meant if he wasn't alive to do so, then his daughter would have lived. He even gave himself two months to contemplate this alternative, when he granted his daughter's wish to tie up all her loose ends, before he would finally sacrifice her. At any point during those two months, he could have willingly given up his life, realizing he was not the most important being in the universe and God would have accepted that, taking his own sacrifice instead of his daughter's. But he couldn't do it. He considered himself too important and his daughter's of far lesser value. He would rather sacrifice his daughter than himself. Now you tell me, what kind of man would make that choice? What kind of father was he, willing to preserve his own life over that of his daughter's."

"Suicide is a crime against God," Pearce proclaimed.

"Perhaps in your religion, but not in mine as long as you have someone else do the killing for you. Masada certainly provided enough evidence of that. His own vanity and self-importance are what caused the death of his daughter. Hence using God's name in vain in an oath that was only intended to serve his own glorification. He did have a choice and would have been far more respected in making the right one."

"I think I see it now."

"Anyhow, you got me completely off track, but all I was trying to point out was that Christianity lacked the legitimacy of being the true defender of God's will. That's why it is essential to demonstrate that Revelation is really a Hebrew prophecy that ranks right up there with all the other ancient prophecies."

"Well, thousands of people that let themselves be martyred for their Christian faith would like to disagree with you," he asserted his opinion. "They obviously thought their faith was a completely legitimate reason to die."

"I've certainly heard that argument before and all I can say is that it's absurd. One cannot state that their religion is valid based on the number of people that were willing to martyr themselves rather than deny it. That would be like saying Islam is the true religion because practically every Muslim is willing to sacrifice their life for Allah. But if you really want to know what true sacrifice and martyrdom is, then let's just take a moment to focus on Jewish history. If we assume that the Jewish or Hebraic faith as we know it began with Moses thirty-three hundred years ago when he led about fifteen thousand people into the desert, and we apply the simple rule that a population doubles every two hundred years, taking into consideration losses due to war, famine, disease, then that would mean that in our time, meaning the twenty-first century, there should be approximately one billion Jews on this planet. A number that is supported by the current population of China that had a similar starting date for their civilization. Considering there are less than twenty million Jews currently in the world, then I think if any religion is going to use martyrdom as its definition for being the one true religion, then Judaism has cornered the market on that one. Rather than convert and abandon our religion, we have permitted ourselves to be the world's cannon fodder repeatedly. No other religious group can make that claim to the same degree."

"But you didn't willingly choose to die," Pearce attempted to correct me. "It just sort of happened and it was too late."

"What? You don't think at any time before or after the persecutions that a Jew couldn't make a conscious decision to abandon his faith and adopt another religion in order to live. Of course a few did, but the vast majority chose to remain Jewish and that is why every century the world had more than enough Jews to slaughter without worrying that they would eventually run out of Jews to kill. Six million by the Nazis, ten million by the Ukrainians over a four-hundred-year span, two million over four wars with the Romans, perhaps a hundred thousand in the Russian programs at the beginning of the twentieth century, the fact is you couldn't keep killing in those numbers for two thousand years unless the majority of Jews continued to refuse to abandon their faith even when offered the choice to convert or die. So, don't bother wasting your breath on telling me that Christians were willing to martyr themselves as proof of their faith and that's why they must have been followers of the true religion. It's simply false and that is verified in lines nine and ten of Chapter 3 in Revelation, which reads *'Behold, I grant some of the synagogue of Satan, of those who say about themselves that they are Jews and are not, but they are lying, behold I shall make them come and worship before your feet and to know that I love you. Because you have kept the word of my patience, I also shall keep you from the trial that is going to come over the entire inhabited world to test all that dwell upon the Earth.'* The first thing that should be obvious to you is that Lazarus is being told that those that have distorted the concepts and teachings of the Torah and pretend that they have inherited the birthright of the Jews are nothing more than ;the children of the Synagogue of Satan. But when the time of judgement nears, some will recognize the were following a lie and beg for forgiveness. You should have realized the first time you read this, that if this truly was Jesus or the Spirit speaking, then why in the world would he say that those returning would worship at Lazarus's feet and come to know he was the beloved of God as it would make no sense because he would have demanded thy worship at his own feet. No sense unless it wasn't Jesus or the Spirit but instead someone like Samuel, saying this to a member of the royal house of David that he himself had anointed for perpetuity a thousand years before. They would worship at the feet of a descendant of David. And if there was any doubt then in sentence 11, Samuel says on behalf of the Lord, *'I come at once, hold fast whatever you have, lest someone takes your crown.'* Once again, ignore the additions of all the churches that these comments are supposedly intended for in Chapter 3 and go back to how the book began with it being a direct conversation between the messenger and Jochanan or Lazarus, as the vision is unfolding before his own eyes, and then how it continues in Chapter 4 with the vision still ongoing. When you read Chapter 1 followed immediately by 4, you recognize that they are structured as one continuous flow and much of what is in Chapter 2 and 3 are merely the editors' additions in an attempt to try and make the book relevant to the various churches by disguising the few nuggets of truth that are in those two chapters. The only message you should garner from these two chapters is that all these Christian Churches, that Lazarus was in some way responsible in founding, were nothing more than the Synagogues of Satan, but Lazarus was now aware of the mistake he had made by contributing to their existence. God promises that if he does not go astray again, and holds fast to his Judaic beliefs, then the crown of David shall be restored to him as his family as a sole inheritance. That would imply that a deliverer from his house must exist at the time of the final battle."

CHAPTER SEVEN: THE BAD

"What do you actually think was meant by the use of the word overcomer John?" I challenged Pearce directly to explain a word that was key to the understanding of my entire proposal that an original Jewish text had been heavily edited and adulterated by scribes within the Catholic Church.

"I don't know what you're referring to Doc," he responded to my question, feigning that he didn't know what I was talking about.

"It's right there in Chapter 3 Sentence 12," I told him. "A strange word to insert in that respect, don't you think.

Pearce recalled his original teaching from Catholic school. "It is implying that some people will have the strength to overcomes the temptations of the world and remains faithful. Those people will be rewarded."

"Really, that is what you think it says. You think they will be rewarded? I believe you need to read that sentence again because it isn't much of a reward if they're to be turned into pillars of stone, trapped for an eternity within the Temple, never to enjoy freedom again. *'And I will make the overcomer into a pillar in The Temple of God and he will not go outside again, and I shall write upon him The Name of my God, and the name of The City, The New Jerusalem, which descends from my God.'* Not only that, but they'll be used as a signpost, having the name of Yahweh inscribed upon them. Not their God, but my God because obviously they weren't true believers. There was an ancient practice of branding the crime one committed into the flesh of their forehead for all to see and know they're guilt. The crime of these overcomers is that they worshipped a false God and that is being made very clear. So, I'll ask you again, what was meant by the 'overcomer' as they certainly weren't an indication that the righteous were about to be rewarded."

"I can't tell you," Peace declined to answer. "That's what I was taught. I can't think of who else they might be."

"I have a suggestion, why don't you grab that thesaurus over there and provide me with the alternative meanings for an overcomer." Pearce did as I instructed and took the book off my shelf and opened to the appropriate page.

He began to read it aloud. "Someone who is victorious, who has come out on top, who overthrew the old order, bested a rival, who is triumphant or managed to subjugate a rival."

"Let's pick the key words out of that. Those that overthrew the old order, subjugated their rivals, claim to be better or the best. Isn't that what Christianity claimed. It claimed to be the replacement to the old religion of the Jews because it was better. Jesus had made them triumphant over their rival, being the original Jewish faith.

I think it is pretty clear who this particular person that is to be made into a stone pillar in the revived city of Jerusalem will be. It will be the false messiah, the false god, the one that the Christians created from a Jewish teacher by the name of Yeshua and called him Jesus. This pillar that resulted in Christianity will be sealed into the rebuilt temple, never to be let loose again, and only the name of Yahweh will be inscribed within the Temple and no other. It is pretty clear from the rest of the Chapter that Lazarus is condemning all the Christian Churches for having preached a false religion and deceiving the people, leading them astray. Notice what he says from sentence fifteen onwards. *'I know your works; you are neither cold nor hot; because it is necessary that you be either cold or hot, and you are lukewarm and neither cold nor hot, I am going to vomit you from my mouth. Because you said that you are rich, and, 'I have prospered, and I lack nothing', and you do not know that you are sick and wretched and poor and naked, I counsel you to buy gold from me, proved by fire, that you may prosper, and white garments to put on, lest the shame of your nakedness be revealed, and eye salve to apply that you may see. I rebuke and discipline those whom I love. Be zealous therefore and return.'* That's pretty severe and harsh, condemning those that he had contributed towards making them think of themselves as greater, but now all he wants to do is rid himself of their pride and smugness by vomiting them out."

"But those comments were only intended for the Church of the Laodiceans," Pearce argued. "Not for all the Churches.

"Wasn't it," I grinned. "The original warning is clearly stated in sentence thirteen where he says the spirit of Samuel is passing on this warning to all the churches. Notice that sentence fourteen is completely out of place in both style and writing, referring to the angel of the Laodicean church and thereby a feeble and false attempt to limit the accusation just to them. Lazarus is relaying Samuel's message that all the churches are to be condemned. There would be no half-way worship of Yahweh tolerated any longer. There could be no concessions to paganism in order that the churches could continue to worship a man as being a god, no matter how you tried to argue he was somehow in the middle. Either you do worship the one God, or you don't, there is absolutely no middle ground, or lukewarm as Lazarus prefers to describe it. But the Church was countering his condemnation by saying they have grown in size and are prospering and therefore there was no reason to change what they were preaching. Lazarus concedes that may be true, but they would only prosper in the future from practicing the one religion that has already been tried by fire and approved by God, which was Judaism. They must repent now before it is too late, he warns them. They are all blind to the truth and need a salve in order to open their eyes to reality. Sentence twenty is an indication that Lazarus will welcome back anyone that returns to the true faith, but the next sentence is an obvious addition from a later editor, because where it is Lazarus speaking in the first person, he suddenly becomes Jesus in this sentence, only to switch back to the first-person Lazarus in sentence one of Chapter 4. You have to admit John that this was a poorly constructed insertion by a later editor, because it is so obvious that the speaker being Lazarus suddenly changed."

"It might appear that way," Pearce admitted, "But as I was taught, Jesus was speaking though John at that moment, so at any point the first-person speaking could have been either John or Jesus."

"Are we now talking about a possession here John, because that is what I think you are suggesting. I know you believe that demons can possess a body and speak through them but now you're telling me that Jesus could do the same. I'm not buying it!"

"That's how it was explained to me," he replied calmly as if it was something you could see happen every day, so why doubt it..

"Well, I'm glad to see that at least someone in your school was asking questions but just remember this, if Jesus was able to take possession of bodies the same way you believe demons do, then he could have done so any time over the past two thousand years since John and made certain that the world didn't go to hell during all that time. But he didn't and that should tell you the obvious, that he can't. Everyone that has claimed to be Jesus, has been locked up in an asylum because they weren't him."

"How do we know that some of them really weren't possessed by the spirit of Jesus," Pearce questioned. "But we refused to listen and that's why they were locked away."

"Really John? The son of God couldn't find a way to convince people that he returned and simply allowed us to give some poor man he possessed to suffer through electroshock therapy. Hardly the behavior I would expect from a deity. Maybe you want to believe Lazarus was the exception and he could switch back and forth between his own personality and that of Jesus but I'm not willing to believe that and I'm guessing a lot of others aren't about to accept it either. Why don't we just agree it was a later addition as the Church editors tried to salvage the chapter which was obviously a condemnation of all the churches at the time by Lazarus. Plain and simple."

"But that's not true," Pearce argued.

"I'm only reading what is there, John. Agree with me or don't agree, either way I can only describe what I see in print. The same way that I see from the beginning of Chapter 4 that it is Lazarus' voice that is speaking and no other. *'After these things I saw, and behold, a door opened in Heaven, and a voice which I heard like a trumpet speaking with me saying, "Come up here, and I shall show you whatever is granted to happen after these things." And at once I was in The Shekinah, and behold a throne fixed in Heaven, and upon the throne sat He; And He who sat was as the likeness of the appearance of Jasper red quartz stone and of red and white Sardius, and a rainbow of the clouds which encircled the throne was like the appearance of an emerald; And around the throne, twenty four thrones, and upon those thrones, twenty four Elders who sat wearing white garments and crowns of gold upon their heads.'* Pretty impressive but I should let you know that the description bears a striking resemblance to how Ezekiel described the throne too in his vision."

"I don't recall my text mentioning the Shekinah," Pearce questioned my choice of words. "It says he was in the spirit."

"And you believe that actually makes sense when your version used the word 'spirit'. I don't want to sound facetious John, but which spirit did you think he entered. The holy spirit, the holy ghost, or was it some other kind of spirit. How does one even enter into another being? I have to know how that works, if I'm to accept your wording in the King James version. The issue, in case it's not obvious to you, is that the Aramaic refers to the Shekinah, but the Greek language has no concept by which to translate the Shekinah. How Christians could have continued to use the word spirit for the past two millennia, even though you can see it makes no sense, is beyond me. You can't enter into a spirit, but no one has ever bothered to find out what was meant by it or how that wording came into existence. But the Shekinah, that's a completely different story. The cloud in which God resides when he manifests himself while on earth, where all souls initiate from when we are born and return to when we die, that is an alternate dimensional space that can be entered into, just as Lazarus describes."

"So, is that like heaven?" Pearce asked.

"No," I answered firmly. "In the original Jewish beliefs, there was no heaven and there was no hell. There was only the Shekinah. Those concepts of either ascending into heaven or being cast down into the pits of hell came much later after the exiles that were in Babylon returned to Israel. If anything, the Shekinah could be considered to be an energy pool and in that case you would enter oblivion."

"Sort of like entering into the light," Pearce proposed.

"More like becoming part of the light," I answered. "The concept aligns with modern science, in that energy cannot be created nor destroyed but is recycled and that there is a constant transmutation between the physical state and the energy state throughout all of time. I know, when I leave this plane of existence that I'll be returning to the Shekinah. I'm not suggesting to you that the concept is as comforting as thinking there's going to be a resort vacation lounge where you lay back on a couch surrounded by all your past friends and ancestors, while strumming a harp but really, from my point of view, when I leave this life, I don't really care.

That is why I have known practically from the day I was born, that I had a set number of years in order to make an impact and see that my life actually added value to this world. You want to know the meaning of life, John. That's it. That is why we are here, John. We are here to make a difference and we can see that message loud and clear from the Old Testament. All those people in the bible existed for only one reason and that was to change the world. Thy did it and we should emulate them. And Revelation is clearly based on the Old Testament. The 'He' of which Lazarus speaks of, sitting on the throne is Yahweh. Notice that his description of the Almighty is without form, a myriad of brilliant colors, stones that reflected the essence of fire and ice simultaneously, with mists of green clouds revolving around these central flames. It is a beautiful image filled with power and awe, the essential spiritual concept of Yahweh, but notice there is absolutely no mention of his seeing Jesus. There's no second throne that is positioned on this dais. It's a single throne. And before you say something, I already know that Christian apologists insist that Jesus's presence is implied, but Lazarus is providing an image that is clearly black and white, despite all the color references. Now regarding the twenty-four elders, I will remind you that when King David initially set up the temple priesthood, it involved rotating the existing twenty-four Aaronic families through the position of the High Priesthood. This is a specific reference to the elders of these priestly families and has no relations to the concept of the seventy judges appointed by Moses or the seventy members of the Sanhedrin. This is clearly a reference to the Aaronic priesthood and the Christian concept of Jesus being the last high priest has absolutely no bearing to this vision. These twenty-four are still active and playing a role that is maintained in heaven, just as it was done on earth. And let me mention it again, there is no reference at this point to Jesus at all."

Pearce was silent for what seemed like minutes. As much as he may have wanted to express a counter argument, the reality was that he couldn't think of anything to say. "I'll have to read that chapter again," was all that he could mutter in a stifled voice that was barely audible.

"Well, while you're reading it, pay attention to sentence five and what follows afterwards. *'And from the throne proceeds thunders and lightnings and voices, and seven lamps were burning before that throne, which are The Seven Spirits of God. And before the throne, a sea of glass as the likeness of crystal, and in the midst of the throne and around the throne, four beasts that were full of eyes, front and back. The first beast was like a lion; the second had the likeness of a calf; the third beast had a face like a man and the fourth beast, the likeness of a flying eagle. Each one of these four beasts stood and had from its appendages and over it six surrounding wings, and from within they are full of eyes and are not silent day or night, saying, "Holy, holy, holy, Lord Yahweh, Almighty, who was and is and is to come.'* I've already talked about the seven menorahs but the seven spirits of God are introduced but Lazarus fails to explain what he is actually referring to because he expects his readers will automatically know from where he's taken his reference from."

"We have an explanation for the seven spirits in our beliefs, Doc."

"No, what you have is a desperate attempt by Christian leaders to try and answer what these seven spirits are, but they have no conclusive answer, because the seven lower Sefirot, were an ancient Judaic concept that specifically related to the qualities of divine interaction in our world. These are Chesed, meaning loving-kindness, Gevurah implying strength or justice, Tiferet regarding both beauty and harmony, Netzach referring to eternity and endurance. Hod the pursuit of splendor or glory, Yesod which is the foundation of existence, and finally Malchut which is recognizing God's kingship and sovereignty over the universe. It is perfectly clear that these attributes describe how God expresses Himself in our world and it is intended that the characteristics will be mirrored within our own human behavior as viable aspects of spiritual growth and ethical conduct. They also reflect the connection between the divine and the created world, offering a framework for understanding how humans can interact with divinity by emulating these qualities. If anything shouts to you that this book is a Jewish document, then this certainly does!"

"What about the creatures holding up the throne," Pearce asked. "Can you explain those as well?" Pearce scoffed merely at thinking I would try to explain what he considered inexplicable.

"Actually, I can," I responded calmly. "Read Ezekiel and you will see the beasts are very similar to those he describes but the essential features are all based on the Seraphim that were standing in the Holy Temple. The Seraphim were composites of these beasts. The chimera of the Seraphim has been separated into their individual components, because each beast on its own is capable of great power. Each proclaims the eternity of the Lord, who was, is and will be, but only in the singular, implying that there is no one other than God that has that eternal quality. There is no reference to any other deity. This is confirmed in sentence nine where Lazarus says, 'And when these four beasts give glory and honor and thanks to Him who sits upon the throne; to The One Living to the eternity of eternities, amen.' It doesn't say to Them or to a Trinity. There is only the One Living God and there isn't any reference to The One and His Son. Wouldn't you think that would be a major oversight if this was a Christian document?"

"Well..."

"It was a rhetorical question, John. The obvious answer is that it's not a Christian document. Sentence eleven also confirms that there is only the one God, and it is He alone that was the creator of all things. This was a clear message to the Mineans and other Christians that they were wrong for initially supporting the movement that broke them away from Judaism.

"But what about the lamb that opens the seals of the book in the next chapter," Pearce asked. "Doesn't that tell you that Jesus was the son of God?"

"Let's say for your sake, it was Jesus. What was his task?"

"What do you mean?"

"What I just asked. What was the purpose of introducing this individual in chapter five?"

"To open the book, obviously," he answered. "No man could open it, so it had to be someone more than a man. That's why it was Jesus," he insisted.

"So, you can honestly say that it was necessary for there to be a Jesus in order to release the four Horsemen of the Apocalypse. Without Jesus, that evil that they bring could not be unleashed on the world. War, pestilence, famine and massive death are going to be released upon this world because Jesus is going to bring it about."

"No, that's not what it says!"

"That is exactly what it says," I corrected him. "In fact, he opens the fifth seal and that's all about vengeance. The sixth seal screams out for the unleashing of an end of the world catastrophe. Earthquakes, total blackout of the sun, a blood moon, asteroids colliding with earth, the collapse of mountains and the sinking of islands. Well thank you Jesus for bringing that all about. We couldn't have done it without you. So much for love and forgiveness; instead, he is the harbinger of death. It certainly paints a very ugly picture of Jesus, if this is his main purpose, to bring about the destruction of our world."

Pearce's mouth dropped open as I described the doomsday that would be wrought upon the earth by the one being he proclaimed could open the seals as it went against every teaching that he had been raised with concerning Jesus. There was no love displayed in this chapter. No mercy or forgiveness. There was just incredible hatred for mankind. Once he was finally able to find his voice, he attempted to make an excuse for the destruction created in the name of Jesus. "There has to be a cleansing. Because the world has become so evil, there is no other way to free mankind from sin other than to destroy mankind."

"I thought he died for your sins, and all was forgiven, isn't that the fundamental belief of Christianity."

"It is," Peace agreed, "But first you have to accept Jesus into your life in order to be forgiven."

"And if you don't, then you're going to die a miserable death from the horrors that he unleashes upon the earth. Isn't that what is saying?"

"It's not really saying that. It is only saying that because of the sins committed by the populace, God has no alternative but to release the four horsemen in order to cleanse the world."

"That's not what it says. It says that this seven horned, seven eyed creature seizes the book out of God's hands, then the beasts and elders, numbering over a hundred million, all submit to him and bow down, proclaiming that they will now receive power as kings and priests to take over and reign on earth. This sounds like a flashback to the power struggle between Lucifer and Yahweh that is suggested in Isaiah 14:12-15 and Ezkiel 28:12-17."

"You're suggesting the lamb is actually Satan," Pearce caught my insinuation.

"The Aramaic word for a goat is 'tsaphiyr' pronounced more like tzfir. You know what's really interesting. They use the same name for a sheep. That being the case, the original story before the editors got hold of it could have been about a multi-horned, multi-eyed being that wrestled the box from the hands of Yahweh, and in so doing, many of the celestial beings decided to follow this challenger to God's power. I think you are well aware of who would be referred to if they had used the word goat. Influenced by Babylonian culture multiple horns and eyes add a sense of distortion and chaos, suggesting that demons exist beyond the boundaries of the natural world. Horns amplify their power and aggression, while eyes imply an unsettling level of perception or intelligence, qualities often attributed to supernatural beings. These features emphasize that demonic creatures are unnatural, alien, and frightening, existing outside human understanding. This being the case, it becomes fully understandable why this being, who is not Jesus, as you have been taught, opens the seals. It is so he can sow chaos and destruction in our world."

"I need a break Doc," Pearce pleaded. "This is all a bit too much for me to take in all at once."

"A break is a good idea, John. Let's take a rest for a while.

Peace looked relieved.

"And if you're going to get up and take a break, John, let's get another pot of coffee on the boil."

"Anything else you'd like," Pearce snapped back at me.

"Cookies, but I don't think I have any. Check the cupboards anyway."

CHAPTER EIGHT: THE UGLY

"Okay, that's enough of a break," I decided. "Time for us to get back to business." Pearce did not look too eager to reconvene the conversation.

Chapter seven also makes it very clear to whom the book was being directed. In case you didn't pay attention to it at first, the hundred and forty-four thousand that are to be rescued from the destruction are selected from the twelve tribes of Israel. That means that it is God's intention to rescue the Jewish people at the End of Days."

"But that's impossible. You don't know any longer who is from which tribe any longer," Pearce insisted. "Ten of the tribes got lost. It can't be done. So, you are definitely mistaken on that one, Doc!"

"Are you actually saying that God doesn't have the power to bring together all the tribes of Judah. How can you as a Christian on one hand claim that God has the ability to establish his progeny in human form but doesn't have enough power to find twelve thousand descendants from each of the 'so-called' lost tribes. I would think that would be child's play for Him."

"You can't find what no one even remembers," Pearce insisted.

"But God is omnipotent, isn't He? He remembers everything. Anyway, what you're saying is not entirely true," I corrected him. "Many don't know which tribe they were affiliated with, but at the same time, many do as well. I certainly know that I am descended from the tribe of Levi. Saul of Tarsus knew he was a Benjaminite, which meant that his direct relatives were as well and their descendants probably have retained that memory. James the son of Alphaeus was from the tribe of Zebulun. There's no reason to believe any of the descendants of his relatives would forget their tribal origins. The same is true for the relatives of the apostle Nathanael, known as Bartholomew, who descended from the tribe of Naphtali. Or Simon the Zealot from the tribe of Issachar. James son of Zebedee, an Ephraimite of the tribe of Joseph. Simon bar Jonah, a Reubenite. Just because the fall of the northern kingdom of Israel is described as an obliteration of their existence as a monarchy doesn't mean that people erased from their memories their tribal affiliations. And if they hadn't forgotten their roots by the time of Jesus, over seven hundred years after the fall of the Northern Kingdom, then there's no reason to believe they're going to do so even two millennia afterwards. But there's another interesting detail about that tribal list provided in chapter seven."

"What's that," Pearce asked, somewhat less enthusiastically than I had expected. It was obvious he was not enjoying my lecturing him on his own religious beliefs.

"No tribe of Dan. That tribe was replaced by Manasseh, which was just another way of saying a tribe belonging to Joseph."

"What's the significance of that?" Pearce wondered.

"One day I'll write a book about it but my thoughts on the matter is that the tribe of Dan had essentially settled in new lands around the time of King Solomon. In the original division of Canaan, the Danites were given a very small track of land with no river access except around the port of Joppa and bordering the north boundary of Philistia. That is why you find Samson constantly involved in either loving or fighting the Philistines. It was far from being an equitable division compared to the other tribes. Fortunately, the Danites tended to be seafaring people, just like the Greeks that had settled in Philistia. Solomon took advantage of their skill and sent them sailing throughout the Mediterranean and far beyond as he established a huge network of trade and commerce. It is said they ventured far beyond the Pillars of Hercules and may have even settled to a large part in Ireland.

"Why would scholars suspect that.

"A large number of villages and towns were incorporated with the name of Dan in them. One can assume it was a coincidence, but as you know I will tell you, there are no coincidences. With most of the tribe migrating to places like Ireland, Sepphoris or Carthage, they eventually became a non-entity in Israel and were lost to the tribal confederacy. An interesting fact is that Hippolytus of Rome, at some time in the third century AD wrote that he expected the Antichrist to arise from the tribe of Dan."

"That doesn't seem strange to you?" Pearce questioned how an ancient tribe of Israel could essentially become anti-Semitic."

"This was likely based on some ancient traditions that the Danites would sever their relations and actually turn against the rest of Israel, which is exactly what appears to be happening with Ireland's political stance right now. Of all the European nations, Ireland has become the most hostile anti-Israel country among them. That again cannot by coincidence. Another reason why I believe the End of Days that Lazarus prophesized is about to happen."

"But that chapter also speaks of the great multitude that showed up in white robes from all the nations of the world and shouted praise to God."

"The original rendering was likely that that prayed and pleaded for their own salvation because they saw they were being left behind, while the Jews were being saved, and this didn't sit well with the later editors. How could the followers of Christ possibly be left behind? From a totally Christian viewpoint, that couldn't be possible. The editors had to make an addition that told the people that Christians would be save too. I believe that the original chapter went from sentence 8 directly to sentence 11 and then ended with sentence twelve. Sentences 9 and 10 are definitely an insertion, as you can see they appear entirely disjointed because the topic at hand should actually be followed by sentence thirteen but the editors couldn't have the angels saying Amen without introducing this Christian throng because Amen infers a conclusion to the event. They had no choice but to insert it, even if they did so awkwardly, before saying Amen."

"You don't believe that a true Christian believer will be saved?"

"Remember what was prophesized," I instructed him. "The fourth horseman is going to kill with the sword tainted with disease and hunger over a quarter of the earth's population. That's over one and a half billion people. Even if you think all that death is going to occur among those populations perceived as the enemies of God, then there are going to be a lot of Christians that die as well to meet that large a number. That is the nature of war, and it only ends when the suffering is greater on one side than the other and that side with the higher incidence can no longer tolerate supporting the war effort. When you read the book properly, you'll see that it gets really ugly when you delve deep into chapter eight. Rather than perceiving the storyline as if it were the angels waging this destruction of the earth, but instead understanding it to be an agenda that has each event heralded by the sounding of a trumpet, then it begins to make a lot of sense. The first trumpet is the unleashing of the nuclear weapon arsenals on both sides. It's represented as thundering, lightning and a trembling of the earth. Exactly how we would perceive the instant a nuclear warhead to be as soon as it explodes. The radioactive cloud falls upon the people like a mixture of hail and brimstone, the intense radioactivity burning everything in its wake, including the forests and the grass. The second trumpet heralds the devastation as the earth reacts to this unleashed power with a series of quakes and eruptions, because it will be the nuclear reactors that are first targeted, and they set off a chain reaction that now floods the seas with poisonous radiation that kills a third of the creatures that live in the oceans. As if that wasn't enough, there is another weapon, fired from the satellites that orbit the earth, seen as a bright light that burns and vaporizes all that it encounters. If you don't think such weapons exist, then just remember how there was a bright light that witnesses claim shone down on Lahaina, on August 8th before that part of Maui was obliterated, but strangely only those homes and businesses that seem to have been owned by the indigenous population. As such, not only does this third trumpet herald the use of laser weapons but by this time a third of the fresh waters of the earth have become contaminated and undrinkable causing widespread death and suffering. By the fourth trumpet the nuclear cloud has become so thick that the sun and moon appear dimmed to a third of their normal brilliance, and at most there appears to be four hours of sunlight during the day. You would think that would be enough devastation and punishment, but Lazarus is taunted by eagle who with its cries of woes is in all likelihood proclaiming that 'you ain't seen nothing yet.' What was to come would be even worse."

"You mean an angel," Pearce tried to correct me.

"No, I mean an eagle," I insisted. "The King James version is the only one that says it is an angel, because the royal translator made a mistake. It is definitely an eagle that is screaming the worst is yet to come."

"Why an eagle?" Pearce sounded confused.

"Haven't you figured out by now why the animals mentioned as participants in this end of the world affair are described as bears, dragons and eagles? Stop thinking of them as animals and start thinking of them as countries."

"Oh…" was Pearce's immediate response as if suddenly donned on him which countries they represented.

"The eagle is saying it will retaliate. Is that correct?"

"Whether the response is offensive or defensive, the war is going to get far worse. It is inevitable."

"Can't see how things could get much worse," Pearce commented as he pictured the devastation that had just been described.

"I'm certain you read the book before. Five months of torture to the point of wishing you were dead. It does sound like there are fates worse than death," I responded. "Whether these are mutated insects that were affected by radiation from the bombs, or some previously unknown species that lived in the bowels of the earth but found a means to escape to the surface due to all the fissures created in the Earth's crust, the bottom line is we will have no defense against them."

"You certain they're insects? It says in the book that they have a king that directs their attacks. A king with the name of Abaddon. Hardly sounds like insects to me."

"The translation of the name from Hebrew is destruction. It's symbolic in that these creatures serve no other purpose but to inflict torment. The angel of the bottomless pit one can presume is Satan and this would only mean that the insects, or whatever they are, can be considered to be spawned from Hell. But other than torment, and making you wish you were dead; it isn't until the sixth trumpet is sounded that they might finally get their wish granted."

"What do you mean by that?"

"Four angels are loosed from the river Euphrates. Obviously, this is a metaphor because how else would you explain that there are angels bound at that bottom of the river. Instead of the word bound, why don't we replace it with the word allied? If we examine those nations that the Euphrates River passes through, then there's Turkey, Syria and Iraq. But what we need to realize is that when the bible made reference to the Euphrates it was in the context of the Euphrates-Tigris River basin. There are tributaries that feed into the Euphrates that originate in Iran as offshoots of the Karun River. And since demons are merely the flipside of angels, these four nations represent the threat that initiates the war and bloodshed."

Pearce looked confused. "But we're already discussing the sixth angel. The world has already experienced the unleashing of a nuclear holocaust, why then would we refer to them now."

"Look how the sixth trumpet is describing the situation, John. It's a flashback that takes place an hour, a day, a month and a year before the other events, which means it is a reminder to everyone that is still surviving to remember how and where this all started. Of course they couldn't account for all this destruction on their own. That requires support from much larger nations that will carry us into World War III. Who could possibly unbind them and let them loose on the world?"

Pearce remained quiet.

"That wasn't a rhetorical question this time," I finally broke the silence. "I was looking for an answer from you."

"Sorry...I didn't realize...I guess you're waiting for me to say Russia and China."

"You can throw North Korea into the mix as well, now that we know they are sending troops to fight against the Ukraine. The triggers are in place but what we don't know is when that countdown is set to begin. But we can see from the alliances that the time must be close. We can see Putin already puffing up his chest, and the Ayatollahs crowing loudly. Now that Israel and Iran are in direct conflict with one another, I can only think that the clock is about to start ticking. Sadly, most people don't even realize the significance of an alliance between Russia, China and Iran and I'll even throw in Turkey, though it still continues to pretend it is a western nation and allied to NATO. This Gang of Four corrupt and soulless nations, are dedicated to see the end of western civilization as we know it."

"If only we knew when all of this was going to begin in earnest," Pearce sighed.

"Perhaps we do," I exhaled. "Perhaps we do."

CHAPTER NINE: THE NUMBERS GAME

"I thought by now you would have realized that the numbers provided in the chapters from Revelation are key to unlocking the mystery as to when it all begins. They weren't selected at random. Numbers are the universal language of man. They overcome barriers of language, distance and time. They are unalterable and convey simple truths as long as we have the ability to see their significance. Do you remember in my articles on Rediscovering the Exodus, #6 and #8, in which I reveal how Moses used numbers to tell us not only about his identity but about the beginnings of Israel as a people. People often ask who is a prophet, or why should we believe someone has the gift of prophecy; and the answer is quite simple. Those with the particular gift see the patterns, the numbers, the evidence that is strewn across all of our paths, but sadly we are unable to see them. They identify with the patterns in the sky, the leaves, the blades of grass, things that we see every day of our lives, but we don't recognize. That is the true nature of prophecy, the ability to see clearly what has always been there but which the masses are blind to identifying. We just have to figure out what Lazarus was observing and then we'll have our answers."

"You think it is buried in the numbers he uses," Pearce sounded somewhat skeptical.

"It should be obvious to anyone that he was playing the numbers game. The simple fact that he waits until chapter seven before revealing the events at the End of Days is a message all by itself. And in case you haven't noticed, the most repetitive number in this book is the number seven. It is practically everywhere you read, constantly being strewn throughout almost every chapter. But does anyone pay attention to what Jochanan or Eleazar is attempting to convey when he makes use of this particular number? Probably not, because as I just said, the average person tends to overlook the obvious."

"I noticed it," Pearce immediately tried to correct my statement and suggest that he was attuned to the evidence.

"Perhaps you did John, but did you also understand what his intentions were for repeating the number?"

"I was working on a theory."

"Good, when you finally think you figured it out, let me know. In the meantime, I will tell you about my thoughts on the matter."

"Which are your thoughts and not necessarily everyone else's," he quickly reminded me.

"True," I agreed, "But since this is my story, right now those are the only thoughts that count," I stated with a slight smirk and laugh. "It is Lazarus's way of telling me, who he was, by birthright and who he remained or wanted to be remembered as, at time of his death. The voice in my head only urged me to read the book and discover for myself why it was important, but it was Lazarus's repeated use of the number seven that proved that he was writing specifically for a particular population. And in case you don't know, that was his people, the Jews, and not the Christians that adopted the book as their own much later. The symbolism of the number was patently obvious, and it was why Akiva mistakenly thought the book was written for his time. Had Akiva taken the time to focus on some of the other numbers used throughout the book, he would have come to the realization that it was not about his time at all. That mistake cost us close to a million lives."

"Would you like to explain the significance Doc. So far, you're only telling me that the mention of 'seven' was meant to be significant but you haven't provided any details," Pearce stated impatiently.

"I was getting to it," I assured him. "You agree with me that the number does appear to be highlighted throughout the book of Revelation, I will now tell you another fact, that the number seven is the cardinal number of Judaism. Right from the beginning of time, and I mean that literally, as we can personally witness from the first verse in the Old Testament which contains seven words."

"Wait a minute," Pearce interrupted me. "That's not true. In the beginning God created the heaven and the earth is ten words."

"In English but not in the original Hebrew. Bereshith, 'barah Elohim, et ha-shamayim, v'et ha-eretz' is only seven words. And then the chapter goes on to say that the world was created in seven days. Furthermore, day seven is to be treated as a holy day or the Sabbath, a day to recognize and pay homage to the God of the Jews."

"Having seven days in a week isn't exactly a big deal, Doc. It just happens to be par for the course."

"Oh John, you should have paid more attention in history class. The Romans had nine days in a week. The Babylonians also had a unique structure for their weeks which only consisted of five days. The ancient Egyptian week consisted of ten days. As you can see, the concept of a seven-day week was essentially unique and specifically pointed to being a Jewish development. But there is far more to the number seven in the Jewish religion than just the number of days in a week. The Shmita years are all based on 'seven' with the freedom from servitude to occur in or following that seventh year. Plus, there was a requirement for Jewish farmers to let the land lay fallow during the seventh year as instructed by Leviticus 25:4. After seven cycles of Shmita, Judaism has what it refers to as the Jubilee year or Yovel, which is described in Leviticus 25:8. As you can see, our entire system of determining the holy periods and intercalating time are based on the uniqueness of the number seven. And yet, there is so much more. There were seven days of preparation for the construction of the Tabernacle in the desert according to Leviticus 8:35. On Yom Kippur, the High Priest was commanded to sprinkle the blood in the Temple seven times according to Leviticus 16. The menorah which we've already talked about, Judaism's greatest symbol was commanded by God to be a seven-branched candelabrum. That has been the symbol for Judaism for over three thousand years. Go to Rome and look at Vespasian's arch of triumph and you will see the Romans carrying the menorah as a sign of defeating the Jewish people. The menorah was so important that in Exodus 25:31-40 there are detailed instructions on how it was to be constructed. *'And you shall make a lamp stand of pure gold and there shall be six branches going out of its sides, three branches of the lamp stand out of one side of it and three branches of the lamp stand out of the other side.'* When we hear he number seven, as Jews we spontaneously think of the menorah and then we think immediately afterwards about our ancient Holy Temple in Jerusalem."

"I see your point," John nodded, "But you can't say that a particular number was more relevant to a specific people."

"I wasn't finished making my case yet," I urged him to refrain from making any statements until he heard all the evidence. "Let us not forget that Joshua led the Israelites around the walls of Jericho seven times before the walls fell as read in Joshua 6:15. But you may still be thinking the use of the number is still a mere coincidence Then let's dig deeper and see that Jacob worked for Laban for seven years two times actually, in order to marry his two daughters, Leah and Rachel. That story is in Genesis 29:27 if you're interested in confirming for yourself. But have you ever wondered why there are seven days to the holidays of Passover and Sukkot as dictated in Leviticus 23:6, 34. The festival of Sukkot is known as the "Festival of the Booths", a reminder of the days wondering through the desert after the escape from the slavery in Egypt. That was forty years and to be represented by seven days would appear to be fairly arbitrary unless that number was significant. Leviticus 23:42-42 actually says, *'You shall live in booths seven days in order that future generations may know that I made the Israelite people live in booths when I brought them out of the land of Egypt: I am the Lord your God.'* That is by God's own words that it must be seven days. Why not an entire month? Because He was providing a key, a code to unlock future prophecies, and it was always there for all to see, but so few ever have. Over and over again that particular number has been re-emphasized, such as in our custom of inviting seven symbolic biblical Ushpizin to our Sukkah. Who are the seven Ushpizin you might ask?"

"Actually Doc, I would ask what is an Ushpizin."

"Sorry, I should have used the English. It means patriarchs They were Abraham, Isaac, Jacob, Joseph, Moses, Aaron, and David. The seven men that had the greatest impact on our existence and forged our civilization. On Sukkot we shake seven items in every direction. There is one lulav, one esrog, two willows, and three myrtles. On the seventh day of Sukkot, there is a procession where we will make seven circuits around the Bimah, the platform where the Torah is read. It was always intended that when you think of the number seven, then you'd automatically think of God's holy people. You would know that we are all marked by that number and in any religious document that followed, such as this one by Lazarus. I can go on and on, but the number seven is synonymous with Judaism. And I hope you understand that now."

"Well, an argument could be made for the significance of the number in Christianity as well," Pearce insisted still not willing to accept that the number seven was being specifically used to point towards Judaismm..

"I wasn't finished yet. In a traditional Jewish wedding, the bride is led seven times around the groom. This symbolizes the seven days of creation and now that couple will also create new life. In the second part of the wedding ceremony there are seven blessings recited. Since Yahweh said that we are as a bridegroom unto Him, then these same traditions apply to our marriage to our faith and God. This is called the 'hakafot' but in truth, it was Yahweh's way of ensuring that we would never forget the number seven. Now let me discuss with you the significance of the holy days of Shavuot. Shavuot is celebrated to commemorate Moses receiving the Ten Commandments, on Mount Sinai. These holy days occur seven weeks after Passover as this marks the time that the Jews had departed from Egypt until they received the Decalogue. Shavuot is also a harvest festival. At the time of the Temple, Jews would bring offerings of the first harvest to the Temple in Jerusalem. Farmers were instructed to bring the seven species of grain and produce written about in Deuteronomy 8:8; wheat, barley, grapes, figs, pomegranates, olives and dates. These are the seven species the land of Israel is blessed with. Are you beginning to recognize John, that there is no escaping this simple truth that Judaism is based on the uniqueness of the number seven. As a people, we are tied eternally to that number."

Pearce was about to say something, but I held up my hand for silence. "Shivah is the period of mourning in the Jewish custom. Shivah means seven, as this refers to the first seven days of mourning. So not only is the beginning of Judaism about the number seven, but our personal ending of life is also centered around the same number as well. But so too is our personal beginning, now that I think of it. Seven days you will wait to see if the boy child's life has been blessed and secured, and on the 8th day you will circumcise him. So, we are commanded by God. Those seven days are necessary to receive His blessing of survival. From birth to death our lives are governed by the number seven. I could probably think of more, but I think I should have made my point by now. For the purpose of this discussion, I hope I have convinced you that there was a particular reason the number seven was so frequently used by Lazarus in Revelation. There should be no question that he was aware of this fact and therefore is clearly directing his prophecy to the Jewish population, knowing that no one else would recognize the significance. Now, what is it that you wanted to say?"

"I wanted to say that the number seven plays a role in Christianity as well. You can't just claim that at number is significant to a particular people and no others."

"If that's the case, then tell me how it plays a role in Christianity?" I challenged him to dispute my argument. "Let me hear your supporting argument."

"Well, the fact that God created the world in six days and rested on the seventh is also significant to Christians."

"Only because you took that doctrine from the Torah. Without the Jewish Old Testament, you wouldn't have had any idea about how God created the world. You can't take someone else's beliefs and say they're exclusively your own. But go ahead, give me something else."

"The number seven is often associated in Christianity with divine perfection and completion. For instance, in the Book of Revelation, there are seven churches, seven seals, and seven trumpets, symbolizing the fullness of God's revelation."

"Did you ever go to debating class John? The first lesson they will teach you is that you can't use the subject being discussed as the topic of debate as part of your argument to support your views. That's like saying a dog is a dog because it's called a dog. It just doesn't work that way. And let me comment on your remark of the seven early churches in Christendom. Can you name them?"

"Ephesus, Smyrna, Pergamum, Thyatira, Sardis, Philadelphia and Laodicea." Pearce rattled off their names with a smug smile on his face, as if to say 'aha, I got you'.

"I see you learned your Sunday school lessons well. But what about Rome? What about Jerusalem? What about Antioch, just to name a few others? They were three of the earliest Churches. Don't you think they should have been on the list?"

My response caught Pearce unprepared and all he could do was scratch his head as he tried to think of a response.

"The facts are that there were far more than seven early Churches but in order to fit the context of the story in Revelation, the Church elders shortened the list so it would appear that it was truly a Christian doctrine. They altered the facts to fit the narrative but as you should be beginning to recognize by now, there is no significance to the number seven in Christianity.

"What about Christianity having the seven deadly sins? And don't forget the seven virtues. Those are pretty much Christian concepts!" Pearce shouted in desperation, not certain if he was even correct about what he stated as fact.

"Not exclusively," I advised. "Pride is condemned in Proverbs 16:18. Envy is to be avoided according to Proverbs 14:30. Gluttony is exposed in Proverbs 23:20-21. Laziness or sloth is mentioned in Proverbs 6:6-11. Lust is one of the most addressed sins as can be seen in Exodus 20:14, Proverbs 6:25-29, Proverbs 7, Job 31:1, and is essentially the story in Genesis 39:7-9 concerning Joseph and Potiphar's wife. I have to think about the other two sins. Give me a moment. Oh yes, greed is the same as coveting, so Exodus 20:17 and Micah 2:2, as well as Ecclesiastes 5:10 deal with that subject. And finally, there is wrath, which is condemned in numerous places of the Old Testament; Proverbs 14:29, 15:18 and 16:32, as well as Ecclesiasts 7:9 and Psalm 37:8. You're argument that somehow the seven deadly sins are unique to Christianity is clearly false as once again it was borrowed from pre-existing Jewish doctrine. Would you like me to do the same with Christianity's seven virtues."

"No, I think you've made your point," Peace conceded.

"I hope that you can appreciate the fact that even if Christianity later claimed the book of Revelation as its own, it did not in any way disguise the message being sent mathematically to us over time. That message is that your John, or my Lazarus was always a Jewish prophet and not to be mistaken for any other. But that in no way lessens his message to Christians. It is actually my hope that what I'm writing now, opens the eyes of the Jewish population to read the book and realize we are facing the End of Days unless we do something about it. Lazarus's message needs to be heard by all of us because I am certain it is directed to this time period in human history. It doesn't really matter that the Christian editors in their failing to understanding how solidly grounded the book was in Jewish tradition, that they decided to add sections and treat Lazarus as if he was writing separate letters to each of the Christian Churches in the surrounding region. It was actually a foolish notion when you think about it because, unlike Paul, this Eleazar, Jochanan, or Lazarus, whichever name you prefer to call him, did not have direct connections with all these Churches, as he was in exile on an island in the middle of the Aegean. His book was not about distinct treatises but one very involved storyline that loses its significance as soon as you attempt to divide it into multiple parts and then attempt to courier those parts to separate regions around the Mediterranean. The Christian editors were so busy adding bits and pieces with references to the various Churches and to Jesus, that they completely ignored the fact that numbers played a major role in Eleazar's prophecy. In so doing, they eventually divided the book into 22 chapters, a meaningless number that even confuses present day Christian preachers as to why it had to be so many."

"How can you be so certain it wasn't that many chapters to begin with?" Pearce wondered.

"Because of the language of mathematics once again. Once you are able to appreciate it, then it becomes hard to believe that something so simple, so basic, so easy to detect, is a virtual blind spot to every other person on this planet except to those gifted with this inner sight to recognize the patterns. Lazarus is clear in his message that everything about the number seven is Jewish, and everything referring to seven is good and holy. Had the Christian editors at least had a clue as to what he was communicating, then they would have stopped their editing at twenty-one chapters to try and keep the number seven significant as in the formula of seven times three. But they failed to understand, in the same manner that they failed to appreciate that Lazarus also provided us with a message about the number to be associated with evil."

"He actually provided us with a number by which to identify evil," Pearce sounded surprised as he parroted my words.

"I thought it would have been obvious when you read Revelation. That number is four. As in the four horsemen of the Apocalypse. It is strange that in oriental customs they have always seen the number 4 as a harbinger of death, but it is not until we read Lazarus's book that we realize he has seen something associated with that number that only exists presently in our time and was not in vogue when he wrote his Revelation."

"In vogue?"

"The number initially didn't represent evil. As a matter of fact, biblically, four was not considered evil at all. We had the four corners of the earth, the four winds, it was the day God created the sun, moon and stars to give us light and guidance, these are all good things. But then you jump to our present time and what do we refer to when thinking about the number four. Well, there's the new Gang of Four that has appeared on our world stage, as the axis of evil; Russian, China, North Korea and Iran. We associate mastery of the four elements, earth, water, air and fire with sorcery. The fourth Reich is seen as the goal of the neo-Nazi movements during our lifetime. Did you know that the Chinese People's Liberation Army has structured its military organization around a system that emphasizes four key components, including ground forces, air force, navy and rocket forces. NATO emphasizes four focus areas consisting of deterrence, defense, resilience and crisis management. It is not surprising that the number has now become associated with military operations in our time. And with any military operation there is always going to be death. It's a key number now, but during Lazarus's lifetime, the number had little significance. As such, you have to realize he did not pick it randomly. It's all part of the prophecy."

"You're suggesting we are living in the age of the number four."

"Most definitely. We are surrounded by that number but most of us don't even realize it. Four centuries following Lazarus's death, a Bedouin boy was born that was fated to change the world as we know it and his deadly influence is being felt severely in our own time. Lazarus's message about the four horsemen, the ultimate evil that befalls our planet, is presented metaphorically, but some Christian readers fail to appreciate the symbolism and literally expect there to be four horsemen, which in their mystical reality they visualize demons, to spread the death, pestilence and destruction upon the earth. The prophecy conveys a clear message that we should not look towards demons but instead to a present-day civilization that has built its entire belief system and existence around the number four. In the same way that the number seven represents the Jewish people, then Lazarus is suggesting that this number four will point to the enemies of God. Therefore, we are being advised to discover those people that have the number four imprinted on their hearts, their minds, and their psyche. Those people, that he is referring to have always been in plain sight if only we bothered to read their own literature."

"I know where you're heading with this Doc, and if you're going be Islamophobic, then I can tell you right now that my publisher is not going to accept your manuscript."

"I can understand you are hesitant, John, but is it Islamophobic if I just present facts and let the reader decide for themselves if the number four is an indicator of a potential threat?"

"It is if you suggest that these are events that will take place. It would be like accusing of someone committing a crime, well before they even have that thought of doing such a thing."

"But it's not my prophecy," I argued.

"But it is your interpretation, Pearce reminded me.

"I'm not asking you or anyone else to take my word for it. I'm encouraging everyone to check it out for themselves. They can even discuss it with their Muslim friends whether or not the number four is a key to Islam. Here are simple examples of this universal truth that Lazarus was able to see long before the coming of Mohammad. That in itself should tell you how amazing his ability to prophesize was. One of the most important holy periods in Islam is Eid al-Adha, which lasts for four days, from the 10th to the 14th of Dhul Hijjja. It is the Festival or Feast of the Sacrifice but also called Bakr-Eid. It is celebrated by Muslims around the world each year and it honors the willingness of Abraham to sacrifice his son, as an act of submission to God's command. What's interesting is that it is not an attempt to sacrifice his son Isaac but rather Ishmael. Symbolically, they use this festival to usurp the entire birthright of the Jewish people by claiming it was not Isaac but Ishmael that was saved on the altar and therefore any promises by God afterwards apply to them and not the Jews. The Arch angel, Jibra'il, known to us as Gabriel, stops Abraham from completing the sacrifice. The significance from the numerical aspect is how it is being revealed that those adhering to the number four will attempt to supersede and replace those adhering to the number seven. Is that safe to say John without being accused of Islamophobia?"

"I guess so. It's not as if you're discussing an actual crime."

"Good! I have more to say on the subject. There are four Rashidun or Rightly Guided Caliphs in Islam; Abu Bakr, Umar ibn al-Khattab, Uthman ibn Affan and Ali ibn Abi Talib. It is a common expression amongst Muslims to say, 'Hold firmly to my example and that of the Four Rightly Guided Caliphs'. Whereas in Judaism, we may invite our seven holy men or patriarchs to sit with us in the sukkot as I pointed out earlier, Islam has based its belief around these four.

"Still okay," I asked him.

Peace nodded his head.

"But there is more about the number four in Islam," I continued to explain, "That you are probably not aware of. Did you know that there are only four Arch Angels in Islam, these being: Jibraeel (Gabriel), Mikaeel (Michael), Izraeel (Azrael), and Israfil (Raphael). There are four sacred months in Islam, Muharram, Rajab, Dhu al-Qi'dah and Dhu al'Hijjah. There are four Sunni schools of Fiqh, these being Hanafi, Shafi'i, Maliki and Hanbali. There are four major Sunni Imams, being Abu Hanifi, Muhammad ibn Idris, Malik ibn Anas and Ahmad ibn Ha'nbal. There are for sacred books in Islam, Torah, Zaboor, Injeel and Quran. Whereas, as I have explained we incorporate the number seven into our marriage relationship, the Muslims incorporate four as in waiting four months for those who take an oath for abstention from their wives. The waiting period of the woman whose husband dies is four months. And let us not forget that the Muslim man can take four wives."

"That is a lot of fours in the beliefs," Pearce agreed, "But it could just be coincidence.

"There's far more," I insisted. "Even in their religious tales, they have incorporated the number four. For example, when Abraham wanted to learn the secret of how Allah could raise the dead, they record that Abraham said: 'My Lord, show me how you give life to the dead.' Allah said: 'Why! Do you have no faith?' To which Abraham replied: 'Yes, but in order that my heart be at rest.' Then Allah said: "Take four birds, and tame them to yourself, then put a part of them on every hill, and summon them; they will come to you flying.' As this story points out, there is a relationship between the number four and death. A decision about one's own death could be based on the number four as we see from the events of Surah Taubah that when a conquered people were offered the choice of either conversion to Islam or death, then the 'mushriks', as they referred to these prisoners, had four months in which they needed to consider their choice carefully before responding. Even Shariyah Law has built many of its cornerstones upon the testimony of four witnesses as in this example where someone accuses an honourable woman of unchastity but should he not be able to produce four witnesses, then the accuser will be flogged with eighty, or four times the normal punishment of twenty lashes. During the Uthmanic dynasty there were four main functions present at the court, which were referred to as Shariat, tariqat, ma'rifat and haqiqat."

"Laws based on the number four don't appear to be a bad thing," Pearce suggested.

"I never said the number four was going to be presented as good or bad. Only that it can be associated with a particular people or civilization that uses it repeatedly. Such as Islam speaks of the existence of four worlds, these being, nasut or the world of mankind, malakut or the world of the angels, jabarut, known as the world of power, and lahut or what is referred to as the divine world. The number four practically permeates everything in their culture. The tahlî, consisting of thirty-six different Qur'anic attestations of the divine unity consist of four terms, the first consisting of a negation, followed by that which is actually being negated, then thirdly comes an affirmation and fourthly the One Who is affirmed. And like yourself, there are always going to be those that will insist that the repeated nature of the number four in Islam is nothing more than a coincidence, but I will argue that when that number is tied to the key foundation principles of the faith, and that it did not occur by coincidence but was intentional."

"And if I was to agree that it may have been intentional, then what does that prove?" Pearce still failed to grasp the true meaning of prophecy.

"You do understand the entire point of the book of Revelation, don't you?" I must have sounded somewhat frustrated because I could see that Pearce recoiled from my tone.

"It is to enlighten us as to events that will come about," he responded.

"To enlighten us to events that may come about if we let them happen," I corrected him. "So, if a prophet gives us warning that our future may be endangered by something which hinges on the number four, then don't you think we are being told to look for those things that incorporate the number four that could possibly be the vehicle of that danger? That is the purpose of prophecy after all. This evil let loose on the world will be associated with that number. I've provided you with an example. If you have a better one, then go ahead and tell me about it...Well?"

"Well, what?"

"I'm waiting for a better interpretation," I stomped my foot. "Do you have one?"

"I need to think about it," Pearce declined to answer.

"Well, don't think too long. Time is running out if there is going to be any attempt to thwart this prophecy."

"You still believe that we can stop the 'End of Day's from happening?

"If we don't believe that it is possible then we might as well give up now and all jump off a cliff as if we were a herd of lemmings. Do you really think God would have a prophecy like the one in Revelation if its only purpose was to terrorize us and have us give up hope?"

"Perhaps it is fate," Pearce suggested it was inevitable

"There's always a choice on how we intend to handle what you call fate. We can lay down and accept it or we can challenge it because that is what free will is all about. As they say in the streets, 'use it or lose it'. I'm willing to fight in order to change destiny. Are you?"

CHAPTER TEN: THE FALLEN ANGEL

"Now that I have at least provided a key, being the mastery of the numbers which I explained to you, I think we should take a look into Revelation at Chapter 8 again and use this knowledge of numbers to solve some of the symbolism presented in that chapter. Wouldn't you agree?"

"Let's give it a go," Pearce sounded a little more enthusiastic this time.

"Before I get into any detail, I need you to ask yourself, didn't the book of Revelation appear to go through all these events in Chapters five through seven. Why would it bother to repeat all of these events but in a slightly different manner beginning in Chapter 8? That question should be staring you right in the face about now."

"I never really paid attention to that before," Pearce confessed.

"And that was likely because those that were teaching you in your Sunday school didn't want you to notice it. In the first case, they wanted you to believe it was Jesus, portrayed as one of these seven horned, multi-eyed creatures opening the seals on the books that unleashed unimaginable devastation. But as you will notice in the second version beginning in Chapter 8, it is an angel with an incense burner that unleashes this horrible destruction. How can you have it both ways? And that tells you right away that the church editors were desperate to change the content of the story and to insert Jesus, but in doing so, they made a real mess of it."

"That would mean they split the original narrative on purpose in order to make two differing versions," Pearce deduced.

I clapped my hands in response to his sudden enlightenment. He was finally beginning to see my point. "Sentences three to five of Chapter 8 are actually very interesting when you examine them closely. *'And another Angel came and stood over the altar and had a golden censor, and much incense was given to him to offer with the prayers of all The Holy on the altar which was before the throne. And the smoke of the incense went up with the prayers of The Holy Ones from the hands of the Angel before God. And the angel took the censor and filled it with fire which was upon the altar and cast it over The Earth. And there were thunders and voices and lightnings and earthquakes.'* My version may differ slightly from yours but that is essentially what it says. We don't really use censers anymore, but the basic design hasn't changed for over two thousand years. To fill and operate an incense censer, you first need to prepare the censer by filling it with ash, which allows oxygen to flow around the incense or charcoal freely. Once the charcoal is red-hot, you place a piece of the charcoal into the censer, directly upon the ash, while fanning the charcoal to brighten and enlarge the burn. At all times you have to avoid creating too great a wind which will stir up the ash. The next step is to drop in raw aromatic ingredients like frankincense or herbs directly onto the hot charcoal. Once that is done, you put the lid on the censer and let the smoke come out of the holes on the top of the censer. That is the way it has always been done. So, either Lazarus is witnessing a totally ignorant and clumsy angel, or there is something else happening here. Take note that this was not one of the original angels that was surrounding Yahweh and is specifically introduced as being 'another' or not part of the original gathering. The language used was 'achaer' but this word could also imply a non-believer or someone that does not share the faith. He purposely over fills the burner, producing a tremendous amount of smoke and then even after having placed the incense in the burner does the one thing that should never be done, by placing more red-hot coals on top of the incense. The natural result it that the contents burst into flame and then the angel deliberately casts the censer and the contents onto the earth. One can surmise that Lazarus was witnessing a revolt against God, led by this unfaithful angel, whose entire purpose was to lay waste to mankind. Now go back to the seven horned multi-eyed creature that took the book from God, and do you understand now why I told you Lazarus was indicating it was Satan. By separating the story, the Church editors attempted to make it about Jesus, but they failed miserably. There is no Jesus present in this story and there is no salvation being offered. The events had been set in motion and they could not be stopped."

"If this wasn't ordained by God, then why are the other angels surrounding God blowing the trumpets and as you said earlier, heralding the events." Pearce sounded confused again by my account.

"They are heralding each event but not necessarily because God wanted this to happen. Evil is what evil does. And as I first told you, in the absence of a moral compass and the will to do good, then evil will manifest itself. The shofar or trumpet in the time of the temple was sounded for various reasons. One purpose was to assemble the people and bring them to Jerusalem, which is referred to as Yom Teruah, or the Day of Trumpets. But the horns were also sounded to give warning of impending danger. The trumpets in this case are not bringing about the events as a direct response to their being blown but are giving warning of what is about to happen. Once unleashed, the natural progression cannot be stopped.

I wanted to review these events with you because I want people to realize that what Lazarus was describing in his own terms was not far off from the scale of reality that would afflict the world. He throws out numbers such as a third of this is lost and a third of that, and the number seems so incredible that the natural reaction of people might be to not believe it to be even possible. But there was a study conducted concerning the use of weapons of mass destruction and it was reported that should one hundred bombs of a one megaton fission yield each were to be ignited in major cities of the USA, then the immediate result would be 20% of the population dying, followed by a further 15% after suffering from the burns and radiation poisoning. Therefore, his determination of one third of all life caught in the attack zones is quite accurate."

"Are you implying that Lazarus possessed a degree of scientific knowledge that we only understand now? I find that to be incredulous." Pearce sat there shaking his head.

"He only reported what he believed he saw but I doubt he had any understanding of what he was witnessing. So, in order to deal with the incomprehensible, it was necessary to relate it to the belief system of his time. For example, he's told the falling star's name is wormwood, because it made the waters bitter, which was an attempt to simplify the reality so that he could put it into words that he could comprehend and relate to others. It might not make sense immediately, not until you recognize that wormwood was vital for the process of distilling absinthe, a process discovered in 1789, and had to do with thujone, a ketonic and monoterpene substance found in the wormwood. The chapter had already described mass forests of trees being burnt and this would have released a tremendous amount of monoterpenes, which would then become highly toxic and damaging to our organ systems. The levels of thujone in our waters would be incredibly high.

I've talked about the radioactive cloud blocking out the sun, but it is the number that was affixed to the event, another loss of thirty-three percent of the sunlight that is fascinating. At first glance it would appear that Lazarus is just repeating the number out of convenience but in a report by Dr. Luke Oman on the intensity of the cloud produced by a large scale nuclear war affecting multiple countries, he had calculated that there would be one hundred and fifty million tons of smoke produced from the nuclear fires that would rise above cloud level and effectively block out 70% of the sunlight in the northern hemisphere. A more limited exchange of nuclear weaponry would result in a level of about half that. At half or thirty-five percent, it would be very much in line with the prophecy expounded by Lazarus."

"You're making Lazarus sound like a genius," Pearce gave his opinion on the science. "He couldn't possibly of had any of that information, and even if he did, he wouldn't have understood it. It would be like explaining a car to a caveman."

"I appreciate that you finally called him Lazarus. I thought you were going to continue to call him John or Jochanan for the entirety of this conversation."

"I'm not saying I agree with everything you're claiming Doc, but I will admit you do make some good points. But there's no way he could have understood any of this."

"Exactly, he couldn't possibly understand what he was witnessing, so he expressed it in terms that were relatable to his time period. If you understand that then you'll really like this next one. In sentence thirteen, as I already told you, it reads, 'And I heard an eagle flying in the sky, which said, "Woe, woe, woe, to the inhabitants of The Earth.' As I already told you, it was definitely an eagle and not an angel."

"Is that important?" Pearce questioned. "What difference does it make if it's a talking eagle."

"A huge difference," I instructed. "This is a prophetic vision. Talking animals are always important. If I was to say to you it was a bald eagle, then that would suddenly make an impression on you because then you would think that perhaps it does represent America."

"Yes, if he said it was a bald eagle, then I would think it meant America," he answered.

"Exactly," I concurred. "It's not lamenting about what has happened but what is yet to occur with the sounding of the three remaining trumpets. It's saying that America is now powerless to stop the disasters that are still to befall mankind. The eagle is helpless, incapable of doing anything of preventing the outcome because it failed to take the opportunity to stop the events when it had a chance to do so. Now it has no choice but to retaliate with a weapon of such incomparable magnitude that it resembled a star falling from the sky and practically splitting the earth where it fell. But the response of the eagle takes us into the next chapter and that's why there is this obvious division in the timing of the sounding of the trumpets."

"It's like the ringing of the bell in a boxing match," Pearce drew an analogy.

"If that's how you'd like to think of it, then yes. Rocky has been taking a beating through the first few rounds but he'll come roaring back in the next round."

"Rocky, Doc? Really?"

"You're the one that made the boxing analogy. The next chapter is highly technical. We touched on it earlier, discussing its symbolic nature but when you start breaking it down based on today's current technology then it is absolutely amazing."

"I'm afraid you're beginning to sound like you are enjoying this end of the world scenario too much, Doc."

"Don't misunderstand me. I find it absolutely horrifying but at the same time, Lazarus's ability to describe the events in a such a manner that not only can we visualize them but also relate them to our present-day technology, I find absolutely amazing. You have to remember we're talking about a man that lived two thousand years ago and he is conveying images well beyond his understanding but still in line with our expectations of what nuclear warfare would look like. Yes, I may sound excited because that is astounding!"

"Pardon me if I don't get as enthusiastic about Armageddon, Doc."

"Just look at what was written in Chapter 9. *'And the fifth sounded, and I saw a star that fell from the sky to The Earth, and the key to the pit of The Abyss was given to it. And smoke came up from the pit like the smoke of a great furnace which was heated, and the Sun and the air were darkened by the smoke of the pit.'* You can see it happening when you shut your eyes. America retaliates with a weapon of such magnitude that it gains the upper hand against the enemy, but even so, it is only a temporary relief. The description of how this weapon will not harm any of the vegetation was how they described the effects of the neutron bomb. A specialized thermonuclear device that produces minimal blast damage but releases massive amounts of lethal radiation that has the ability to penetrate through structures while leaving them standing. Forty-eight hours after detonation, troops can already move back into the area without fear of radiation poisoning. Vegetation that was lost will regrow. Back in 1981, Ronald Reagan put the neutron bomb into storage but from what was said forty years ago, was that they were to be released in clusters to blanket an area, much in the way locusts would swarm over an area, but unlike locusts, these clusters have a sting like a scorpion."

"What do you mean they would sting like a scorpion?" Pearce wanted to know. "Explosions blow things up, they don't sting."

"Except that this bomb is all about the radiation sickness, the genetic alteration, the flash burns, these would cause those that didn't die instantly to suffer for months and even years. The illness would seem to be a never-ending torment that would make them pray for death. Lazarus is able to describe exactly what would happen and stinging flesh followed by a venomous illness is probably the best description."

"So how do you explain the next few lines in that chapter?" Pearce was still doubtful.

"You mean where he says, *'And the form of the locusts was like the form of horses prepared for battle, and upon their heads as crowns of the likeness of gold, and their faces were like the faces of men. And they had hair like hair of women and their teeth were like those of lions. And they had breastplates like breastplates of iron and the sound of their wings was like the sound of the chariots of many horses running to battle.'* This is where you realize just how accurate Lazarus can be. Once the initial use of nuclear weapons ceases, as it must because both sides know they would annihilate everything on the planet if they continued, they transition into the more conventional means of warfare. Picture helicopter gunships flying towards you. You can catch glimpses of those sitting in the cockpits, you see their faces underneath their helmets, the whirling blades above them like the flowing hair of women, the guns protruding on the lateral trellises like the teeth of lions, while the thump, thump, thump of the rotors mimics the sound of the horse led chariots charging into battle. Covered in plates of steel from the cockpit to the long-extended tails with the tail rotors resembling the stingers of scorpions. I don't think I would expect Lazarus to describe these helicopters in any other manner than how he did it. His details were perfect. But where his detail becomes unbelievably accurate is when he talks about the enemy's king in sentence eleven. *'And there is a King over them, the Angel of The Abyss, whose name in Hebrew is Avadu, and in Aramaic his name is Shara.'* You don't get more detailed than that."

"I thought you said earlier his Hebrew name was Abaddon, meaning destruction," Pearce questioned my previous statement.

"That's because I knew your version in your personal bible says his Hebrew name is Abaddon, but his Greek name is Apollyon, or something to that effect. Am I correct?"

"You're right, that is what my bible says."

"Because someone much later translated it from the Aramaic and couldn't make any sense of what was written in my version. Lazarus never even bothered to provide the Greek name of their king because he wasn't targeting his book to any Greek readers. What he wrote was this; *'Whose name in Hebrew is Avadu but in the Aramaic is Shara.'* But the church translator couldn't make any sense out of Avadu, so he wrote Abaddon, and since Aramaic wasn't a common or useful language to him, he replaced it with the Greek."

"You're going to tell me what those words mean, right?" Pearce sounded impatient because he knew I was purposely delaying in telling him the actual meaning.

"Of course. The Hebrew translates as 'our slave or servant', but it is the Aramaic which provides a far more accurate meaning, translating as 'one of the faithful' or 'one who has submitted'. And from the look on your face, I can tell you already figured out who those that have submitted are, because it's practically identical to the word Islam which means submission. Now you tell me that Lazarus wasn't blessed with an incredible prophetic ability. Almost five hundred years before the term Islam even existed to describe a particular religious denomination, he's already naming it. Now that the enemy has been identified, it will be much easier to deal with the details of the rest of the chapter and I hope you won't try to level the accusation of Islamophobia at me again, because it's not me saying this but Lazarus. You remember how we discussed the loosing of the four angels bound beneath the waters of the river Euphrates and I told you they were talking about Turkey, Iraq, Syria and Iran. But now that I also explained to you how the number four was an indicator of Islam, I need for you to remember that I also told you that according to Islam, they believe there are four arch angels that are their protectors. It's no coincidence that Lazarus speaks of four angels bound to the people of the Euphrates and according to Islam they believe they have four angels at their beckon call. And of course, as the West has almost always failed to do when it has the upper hand, it does not execute the final killing blow to the enemy, providing them with the time to rebuild, recruit, enlist, and restructure their military as described in sentence fifteen. And the army they rebuild according to sentence sixteen is two hundred thousand-thousand, which is more easily expressed as two hundred million. This number is of particular interest because it would seem almost impossible for the countries mentioned to raise that number of troops, especially after being devastated by nuclear weapons. The population of Iran is ninety million, Iraq forty-five million, Syria twenty-four million and the Muslim population of Turkey, eighty-eight million. Eliminating the aged, children and women from the numbers means that combined, there would only be approximately forty-million available fighters if none were killed during the initial onslaught. Well below Lazarus's prediction of two hundred million. It would be tempting to say that Lazarus was wrong, and his prophecy was therefore faulty if it were not for the fact that he already spoke of the four nations that we identified earlier as the axis of evil. It is calculated that there are at least two hundred million Muslims alone residing in China. Russia only has a population of about fourteen million but the ability for Lazarus to prophesize that even after the first wave of nuclear weapons, the dark forces could still call upon another two hundred million that were likely not involved in the initial attack is incredible. There are those that will still claim coincidence, but the number is too precise and too accurate a reflection of our current political environment and demographics to be a coincidence."

But even though these forces of evil still suffer unimaginable losses, they refuse to surrender as is witnessed in sentence 20 and 21. *'And the rest of the children of men who were not killed by the scourges did not turn from the work of their hands to not worship false gods and idols of gold, of silver and of brass, and of wood and of stone, which do not see, neither hear, nor are able to walk. And they did not turn from their murders or from their witchcraft or from their fornication.'* We have now been made aware that the enemy are not believers in the Judeo-Christian heritage. They come from evil empires than value wealth over life, and in fact are considered to worship death. A death where they are promised the privilege of laying with seventy-virgins as is indicated by their willingness to die for the promise of fornication in their false heaven. A people that still believe in magical beings, such as the Jinn, and consider murder a valued tenet of their religion. Perhaps a people that in their chief religious document, the Quran, call for the death of the Jews, one hundred and nineteen times and a further one hundred and twenty-three verses that call for the fighting and killing of anyone who does not agree with the statement that there is no God but Allah, and Mohammed is his prophet, which can be taken as a directive to slaughter Christians as well. I may have said that Lazarus is writing in particular to the Jews, John, but that doesn't mean he didn't see the danger to Christians as well. You should be afraid, very afraid, and don't tell me it's Islamophobic to say so."

"Not every Muslim wants to see us dead," Pearce defended those that he considered to be good people.

"And not everyone that is religious in any faith, takes God's words literally but there are enough of us that do. And you may want to call someone that follows a god that says to kill the infidels a fanatic, but others will label him as a true believer. And there are enough true believers that take the Quran literally, putting us in danger. Lazarus instructs you to open your eyes and open your ears for a reason. He knows that we will let the media feed us lies and conceal the truth. Tell us how wonderful they are as a people and we're the ones that are intolerant. We have been lied to more this past decade by those in authority than the entire sum of lies for the past century. So, should you be scared? Most definitely, because when you fear those that wish to destroy your world, and everything you hold dear, that's not a phobia, that's common sense!"

CHAPTER ELEVEN: ROLLING THUNDER

"Where was I in our conversation?" I had lost track of the point I was trying to make. We had taken a short break to prepare more coffee and now it was time to sit down again and continue this story.

"I think you were about talk about how you thought the news media outlets have been lying to us and how you think we are being warned about that by Lazarus," Pearce reminded me where I had left off.

"And it is understandable when the Prime Minister of Israel can be accused of being a war criminal and Jews are all practicing genocide. When organizations like UNWRA can hire terrorists onto their staff roles and Jewish students have to fear being attacked when they attend class on a university campus, but those events are hardly reported. Why should they be? After all, it's only Jews involved, and they have always been expendable."

"That's somewhat unfair, Doc. Not everyone is an anti-Semite."

"You mean when a Final Solution, can be chanted in the streets by thousands, shouting a refrain From the River to the Sea, and it can't even raise a headline in the media, even though it's calling for the complete destruction of a sovereign nation that just happens to be Jewish, and meanwhile the United Nations can declare the Wailing Wall to be a historical Muslim site, while at the same time arguing that Jerusalem has nothing to do with the Jews, none of that you want to label as anti-Semitism. It's when you see these events unfolding every day, that's when you know that we are entering into the time Lazarus was describing. That time is upon us and as he calls out, 'For those that have ears, let them see, for those that have eyes, let them hear', if you cannot comprehend the true meaning of his words, then I'm afraid you missed the entire intent of his prophecy. It's not about mythical beasts, it's not about magic. The monsters are real, but they are all wearing human suits."

"You were suggesting that this is only the fourth chapter of the original book?" Pearce was questioning how I had come to that decision.

"Are you trying to change the topic, John?"

"Somewhat. The talk of anti-Semitism makes me somewhat uncomfortable."

"Makes you uncomfortable! Try being Jewish and see how it feels. My wife just told me that it might not be a good idea to tell everyone we meet that I'm Jewish For friggin' sake, we're living in China. Most Chinese don't even know what a Jew is, but they're being told by the government that we're the bad guys in the Middle East destabilizing everything. That's one fifth of the world's population willing to hate you without even knowing what you are because the government tells them to. Try dealing with that one sometime and see how it feels."

"Sorry Doc, I didn't mean to imply that it isn't real. But I really would like to know why you think this is the fourth chapter of the original book."

"Quite easy to explain," I took a deep sigh and switched topics. "In what I identify as the first Chapter, Lazarus introduces himself, Samuel, and the purpose of his being selected for the prophecy. In what would have been Chapter 2, he describes the appearance of Heaven and the throne of God. The third chapter introduce this fallen angel that opens the seven seals and unleashes the final battle, which I have described thus far. And now we come to the fourth chapter, which begins with Chapter 10 of Revelation according to your King James version. The events of the war are now being more clearly defined and we will witness the battle see-sawing between the opposing forces. The hiatuses that are described as occurring during the war are the result of our own naïve beliefs that when our enemies stop firing rockets, then they must be coming to their senses and are prepared to sit around the peace table, rather than accept the obvious that they just ran out of rockets and are waiting for the next shipment to arrive. All this will be clear to you when you read it, keeping what I have just said in mind."

"And this segment of the war is different from what we have just discussed. How are you possibly drawing a dividing line between them."

"Based on the intercession," I stated, thinking it should have been obvious.

"What intercession?"

"This one," I replied. 'And I saw another Angel who descended from Heaven, and he wore a cloud and a rainbow of the sky on his head and his appearance was like the Sun, and his legs like pillars of fire.' The mention of the rainbow is very important, and it has absolutely nothing to do with the Trans movement," I cautioned him not to even attempt to respond to the subject, not even as a joke. The rainbow is the way of God showing his official stamp on what this angel had to say, since he always marked his covenants with man using a rainbow as His particular signature."

"I swear, I wasn't going to say anything about it," Pearce defended himself.

"Good. Just in case, I thought I should forewarn you. Let's continue, 'And he had a small scroll opened in his hand and he placed his right foot on the Sea, but the left on The Earth; And he shouted with a loud voice like a roaring lion, and when he shouted, seven thunders spoke with their voices.' Like everyone else, you probably paid no attention to where he placed his feet."

Pearce admitted that he had given it very little thought.

"Stand up for me John!"

"Why?"

"Just do what I said and get out of your chair and stand up." He did what I asked. "Now take a step." Pearce took a step away from the chair. "Which foot did you lead with?"

He had to think about it momentarily but then answered, "my right."

"As most people will do," I congratulated him. "Now you can sit down again," I instructed. "The angel was no different than us. His first step, using his right foot, takes him into the sea. The second step with his left foot takes him back onto dry land. The prophecy could have said water, but it specifically said the sea, so we know that what is being referred to as an angel is coming from a land across the ocean in order to deliver this message. If we recognize that the battle that had already begun is taking place in the Middle East and possibly Asia, then God's salvation is not coming from Europe or any other connected landmass but is coming from America. Hence, the past reference to the Eagle crying out"

"But these lines speak of a lion."

"But it didn't call him a lion. It only said he roared like a lion. Another way of saying he took on the voice of the lion. There's only one lion in the Middle East and that is the Lion of Judah. It is a declaration that this force coming from across the sea is there to support the Lion of Judah and now they shout in a single unified voice."

"I never thought of that," Pearce admitted.

"There's more. The seven thunders reaffirm that the forces coming are there to save the Jewish people and all the others that remained faithful to God. But the actual thunder that Lazarus hears are the deafening sounds of this giant armada, with its aircraft carriers and warships sailing across the sea. It is the sound of the heavy guns of these ships pounding the enemy's encampments suggesting that the enemy may have already taken over parts of Europe. Lazarus immediately thought the war would be over, but was cautioned not to write down his opinion, as such a conclusion would be premature. The war was still far from over. *'And I heard a voice from Heaven again speaking with me and it said, "Go take the little scroll that is in the hand of the Angel who stands on the land and upon the Sea." And I went to the Angel, and I told him to give me the little scroll and he said to me, "Take and eat it and your belly will be bitter to you, but it will be like honey in your mouth." And I took the little scroll from the hand of the Angel, and I ate it, and it was like sweet honey in my mouth and when I had eaten it, my belly was bitter.'* There are a couple of messages that should be immediately noticeable in this exchange. The first being that there is no intermediary. Lazarus interacts directly with the angel in the same manner that the ancient prophets did. He doesn't require Jesus to instruct him or even intercede. In fact, Jesus has absolutely no part in this entire exchange. But as Lazarus realizes, just as every prophet before him had come to learn, being chosen by God to carry his words can be considered a heavy burden. What should be considered sweet will often earn the prophet the animosity of the common people and those that envy his position. It can make the prophet's life bitter, especially when they must tell the people that two thirds of them will die. It is a tremendous burden but as the angel says to him in sentence eleven, *'And he said to me, "A time is given to you again to prophesy unto the nations and peoples and languages and many Kings".* I know that this version of the Aramaic text reads differently from what you have been accustomed to John, but it is important to pay attention to what was said in the original version. The ability to prophesize is being restored to Lazarus, which means that once upon a time he had the gift but either lost it or failed to use it. Now that he has accepted the fact that he may have been led astray for many years pursuing the cause of the Mineans and has reaffirmed his faith in the ancient Jewish traditions, the gift has been restored to him. But it is also saying that after two thousand years of being misinterpreted as Christina literature, his words must be delivered to all of the diaspora in this twenty-first century, where the Jews have become dispersed across many nations and are governed by many different rulers and speak many different languages."

"Why would he have lost the ability to prophesize in the first place," Pearce questioned.

"Did you know that most of the ancient prophets were from the royal house of David. That was one of the key differences between the other houses that ruled temporarily in Israel. None of those others had the ability of prophecy. But when a prophet becomes a false prophet, then God ensures that his voice is silenced. That's what happened to Lazarus. When he became involved with the development of the Chrisian Church, he lost that ability. There are so many nuances contained within Revelation that are indicators of Jochanan's, as you call him, strained relations with the early Church. What is astounding is that no one picked up on them. Perhaps overlooking them was intentional. Maybe it's natural not to see what you don't want to see. More reason why Lazarus is urging everyone to open their eyes."

"As in not wanting to notice them," Pearce caught the drift of my comment even though I thought I had been pretty clear in my meaning.

"Look at what follows; *'And a reed was given to me like a rod and the Angel was standing and said, "Rise and measure the Temple of God and the altar and those who worship in it, And the inner court of the Temple leave out and do not measure it, because that is given to the Gentiles, and they will trample The Holy City forty two months."'* Notice how the angel is referring to a remnant of the temple, as most of it has been usurped by the Gentiles. And those Gentile nations will trample into the earth what was the most holy of Jewish sites. I'm afraid John by Gentiles, the prophecy is referring to both Christians and Muslims as having permitted our Temple to be desecrated and defamed. Even now the Muslims have erected the Dome of the Rock to stand on what was once the inner court of the Temple. Their mosques have been standing there for just over twelve hundred years,, desecrating the most holy of Jewish sites. You have to ask yourself, as to how Lazarus was able to identify two heretical structures that were built six hundred years after his death on the Temple Mount if he was not gifted with prophetic site."

"I'm actually thinking how could he equate the twelve hundred years to forty-two months. I don't see the connection.

"Rather than call them months, let's call them generations. A new generation is born approximately every thirty years. That equals twelve hundred and sixty years. Remember, terms like days, months, years are all interchangeable when discussing prophecies. It is the number that is significant. Considering both mosques were built between 680 for the Dome of the Rock and 715 for the Al Aqsa mosque, then Lazarus was pointing us to the years 1940 and 1975. You know what happened during that interval, right?"

"You're referring to the Holocaust, the recreation of the State of Israel, and the return of East Jerusalem and the Temple Mount to the Jews."

"Very good, you know your history and you can see how it relates to what Lazarus is saying. He's saying we will rise up again after a great suffering and the

Temple will be returned to us but it has been desecrated and deconstructed for a long period of time by both Christian and Muslim occupation. We must take our time to rebuild, rededicate and decontaminate the abuses it has suffered."

"Does that mean if the Jewish Temple is to be rebuilt, then it should exclude the area that is currently occupied by the Dome?"

"Fair question John," I responded. "The prophecy is saying to measure the Temple of God and the altar area, which would suggest to me that that Dome of the Rock was not built on the exact site of the Holy of Holies. The altar was at the base of the Holy of Holies in the priestly court, which was not the inner court as mentioned by the prophecy. Therefore, it would appear that this most holy and sanctified of areas has not been desecrated. And as for those that still worship in it, I believe was a forewarning that from the time he received the prophecy until it will be actually fulfilled, the Jewish people will have suffered horribly, and there would be retribution against those that desecrated our Temple. The Dome of the Rock has to go!"

"Are you certain that the forty-two months actually refers to the number of generations that will pass before the restoration?"

"Another good question," I agreed. "I know it may seem to you that I pulled that equation out of the air, and I'm afraid I'm going to have to delve into the world of the Kabbalah for his one, as much as I'm against the practice of Jewish mysticism. But again, it shows that Lazarus was prophesizing for a Jewish following, and not the Christians. The number forty-two in Jewish philosophy reflects both physical and spiritual journeys, divine names, and connections to hidden wisdom, making it a powerful number in mystical traditions. As I told you, forget about the reference to days, months or years and just focus on the number. Now you have to understand that Kabbalah was based on ancient Jewish traditions but where it goes wrong is that it believes through its practice you can control the laws of nature. As far as I'm concerned, that's absolute crap. It refers to the forty-two Letter Name of God, which is one of the sacred names of God obviously consisting of forty-two letters and believed to hold great spiritual power. This name is associated with creation, protection, and divine energy and is often recited in certain prayers and meditations. And Lazarus would have been well aware of the Jewish prayer 'Ana B'Koach' which was written in the first century by the sage Rabbi Nehunia ben HaKana."

"An ancestor of yours?" Pearce suddenly interrupted my explanation.

"No. His name is HaKana. My ancestors up to the nineteenth century were Kahana. Two entirely different names. Back to what I was trying to explain to you before you interrupted me. This mystical prayer concealing the name of God consists of seven lines, each with six words. Each word's first letter when strung together forms a 42-letter combination that is used for divine connection and protection and the belief espoused by the Kabbalah stems from this original prayer. Except that the Kabbalistic practice is to use this prayer as a means to connect with spiritual forces. But forty-two is also significant in Judaism because of the number of stops in the desert during the Exodus from Egypt. During their forty years of wandering in the Desert, the Israelites made forty-two encampments on their way to the Promised Land. Each stop represents a stage of spiritual refinement, with the journey symbolizing personal growth and transformation. That same number is now begin applied to the remnant of the Jewish population that has had to undergo a similar spiritual transformation until the time this prophecy is fulfilled, and we rebuild the Temple. So, as you can perhaps now understand, that through the numerology and spiritual symbolism, according to the gematria, which is another way of saying Jewish numerology, the number forty-two represents journeys, growth, and the divine mystery, particularly linked to the mystical aspects of the Torah. A fact which the Christian reader of Revelation would have been completely oblivious to, but just another reason why I can say the book was always intended to be seen as a Jewish prophetic writing."

Pearce was once again stunned into silence. I think I could see his eyes spinning around in his head but then he finally spoke. "I'm even more confused. I never knew any of this stuff, but I still don't see a reference to generations." he excused his lack of knowledge.

"Because it's not what follows the number forty-two that is important. That just provides an indication of time but without being specific. It's the number forty-two that is significant and when it can be applied to a specific situation, that in turn provides the actual time frame."

"That's not how I learned it in Sunday school," Pearce still wrestled with the concept.

"And why would you?" I asked. "Your typical Catholic priest isn't going to yell from the pulpit, 'Hey look at this, I think this is all about some Jewish tradition that Jochanan wants us to follow.' That would certainly be a strike against selling Christianity to the masses."

"Would be a bit of a buzz-kill," Pearce joked for the first time since we engaged in a discussion of the book.

"The next part is interesting too," I dove back into reading the lines from Revelation. *'And I shall grant the two witnesses to prophesy one thousand two hundred and sixty days while wearing sackcloth.'* That would suggest that there would be two other Jewish prophets after Lazarus that are in mourning that deliver a similar message."

"How did you determine they would be Jewish?"

"Based on the numbers again. On average there are 30 days in a month. One thousand two hundred and sixty days is forty-two months. I don't think you need me to remind you why forty-two is significant in Judaism. He's just using the time references of days and months to conceal the prophecy, so that it can only be deciphered by his intended audience. The total number of days makes it sound like a different time period but as you can see, it is the same number that he is repeating over and over again. A distinct message for a Jewish audience and that's why I can say these two prophets are Jewish."

"Any thoughts on when these two witnesses would have appeared.?"

"I'm betting on two thousand five hundred and twenty years after the initial construction of the second Temple."

Pearce glanced at me sideways. "And how did you arrive at that number, Doc? This more hocus-pocus stuff of pulling numbers out of the thin air."

"Not at all," I laughed. "Two prophets, each required one thousand two hundred and sixty days is two thousand five hundred and twenty combined. Since prophecies make little distinction between days, months and years, because a lifetime can be but a single day to God, then in this case, the time that was being referenced could have been years, since months had been used previously. As for the starting point, the interval between the construction of the Holy Temples would be the time frame used."

"So when would that date be?"

"Based on the second temple being completed between 515 and 510 B.C., then that would be the year 2010 A.D. Throw on another six years because the start of our calendar is off by that amount and you're looking at 2016 AD."

"You just magically throw on another six years," Pearce questioned.

"Nothing magic about it. You agree that Jesus was born when Herod was King, right?"

"Yes," Pearce agreed.

"And his birth was two years before Herod died, right?"

"That's what's generally accepted," he nodded.

"But we know now for a fact that Herod died around 4 B.C. The priest that was assigned the job of developing the calendar made a mistake by six years because based on Herod's death, we know that Jesus was born most likely between 5 and 6 B.C."

"So, who are they and how will we know them," was Pearce's next question.

"I believe that becomes pretty obvious with the next sentence. *'These are the two olive trees and the two menorahs, which stand before the Lord of the whole Earth.'* The comparison to the pillars of Jachin and Boaz is too striking to be overlooked. You know that the olive tree is the national tree of Israel. It was olive oil that was used to light the menorah in the Temple. The olive branch in the mouth of the dove meant that God was ready to make peace with mankind again, during the time of Noah. The names of the pillars suggest permanence as in being firmly established and the second is strength. They are a reflection of the Jewish people."

"Yes, yes, that's all fine, but who are they?"

"Assuming they represent two halves of Judaism, then I would think that one is a Rabbinic scholar and the other is a Karaite scholar. These two will reaffirm what was written in Revelation and let it be known that the End of Days is upon us."

"Wait a minute," Pearce held up his hand for me to pause a moment. "You're already making such an announcement, so what do we need these other two for?"

"Let's just say, that if I fulfill the requirement of being the Karaite scholar, and since I began examining the book of Revelation in 2016 as you can confirm from my blog, Kahana's Voice, then I'm guessing that I might be one of those pillars. I don't know who the rabbinic scholar is but I'm pretty certain one will appear that is in agreement with my findings regarding the book. The representation of the olive tree might suggest we are both Kohenim, or sons of Aaron because of the affiliation with lighting the menorah in the Temple."

"And as all your readers are aware," Pearce filled in the gap, "They all know that your family, being Kahana, are all descendants of Aaron. Therefore, you're actually suggesting that you are one of these prophets."

"Perhaps because I'm simply interpreting what Lazarus has already written and that means more of a messenger than a prophet."

"If that's the case, then what's this about you having powers as it describes in sentence six. '*And these have been under the authority to close up the sky that the rain would not descend in the days of those with prophecy, and they now will have authority to change water to blood and to smite The Earth with all plagues as much as they wish.*' Do you really think you possess such power?"

"Not me, per se. But at this point the two mentioned are symbolic of the Jewish people. Strike at either olive tree and Yahweh will inflict the enemy of his people in the same manner that he punished the Pharaoh and the Egyptians in the time of Moses. Today's reality is the IDF. They're already showing what they can do with strikes as far aways as Iran and Yemen. Imagine what would happen if they removed all the restraints which have held them back. But unfortunately, they are being held back, especially by the Biden-Harris administration and that means there will be losses on both sides. And the longer they continue to be restrained, the higher the death total will rise on the Jewish side, because they aren't permitted to put an end to this war, once and for all!" This indecisive stalemate is pretty evident in the seventh sentence. '*And when their testimonies are complete, the behemoth that will ascend from the bottomless pit will make war with them and will overcome them and kill them.*' As far as I'm concerned that sentence is an accurate depiction of October 7ᵗʰ, 2023. Whereas your Chistian perspective sees the bottomless pit as Hell, and Satan as the beast rises out of it, I would view several hundred if not thousand Hamas terrorists crawling out of their tunnels beneath the ground being an equivalent monster. And they did exactly what was described. They overran the towns in Southern Israel, killed around twelve hundred and sixty innocents and took hundreds as captives."

"Twelve hundred and sixty," Pearce repeated the words several times. "Isn't that the number we were talking about."

"As in twelve hundred and sixty days being forty two months. That magical number of forty-two again. Are you beginning to see the connection now John and why that number shows up over and over again"

"But that wouldn't be in the timeline of events that Jochanan is describing," Pearce protested. "Before this he was already talking about American forces arriving from overseas."

"In case you haven't noticed, chronology has little to do with Lazarus's visions. He doesn't follow a linear timestream and I can understand why. He's viewing a panorama of events all playing simultaneously before his eyes. It's as if he's watching several different movies on half a dozen screens simultaneously and trying to connect them all together. So, if he discusses one out of sync with another, it is only because he's focused on all these events at the same time and he's randomly selecting which ones he discloses at any particular time. Look at all these events as if they're happening at relatively the same time frames rather than as linear events. But if you need clarification, then take a look at the next sentence, *'And their corpses came into the street of The Great City, which spiritually is called Sodom and Egypt. And then they of the peoples and generations, languages and nations will look upon their corpses for three and a half days, and they will not allow their corpses to be placed in tombs. And the inhabitants of The Earth will rejoice over them, and they will celebrate, and they will send gifts to each other, because of the two Prophets who tormented the inhabitants of The Earth.'* What Lazarus is describing now is in regard to the captives that Hamas took hostage into their tunnels. It is now calculated that of the remaining one hundred plus captives, over half of them are dead. This doesn't even include those that had died earlier, and Israel had to negotiate for the return of their corpses. The place where their dead bodies are being held without burial s described by Lazarus as a great city, which was referred to as Sodom and Egypt. This again is most likely a mistranslation by the Church editors, the original wording most likely being Sadom of Egypt, which due to their lack of knowledge of ancient Hebrew expressions they would not have understood. that שהדום של מצרים, translates as the footstool of Egypt, which was how Gaza was referred to in ancient times, as one had to cross through the footstool in order to enter along the King's highway into Egypt. But Gaza, which was and is not only an extensive strip of land along the coastline of the Mediterranean, is essentially a single city and referred to as a Great City because of this city-state's nature. It should have been obvious to all, that if Lazarus was making a statement referencing the nature of mankind sinking to the lowest level of morality, then he would have written Sodom and Gomorrah, and we know from the rest of the book of Revelation, he was not one to choose his words carelessly. And in regard to his next line pertaining to the celebration by the rest of the world celebrating the terror that was inflicted upon Israel and their sending gifts, we only have to watch the news to see how true this is with the word protesting against Israel, represented by the prophets and rewarding Hamas with money, land and weapons by which to continue their acts of terror. They're practically singing their praises which is reprehensible. In fact, their openly vile acts of anti-Semitism ,are considered justified and warranted by their imagined acts of torment that they believe the Jewish people have inflicted upon this world. It's ridiculous, but as Goebbel's pointed out, the more you repeat the lie, the more believable it becomes. No truer statement could have been made by Lazarus regarding present-day events than this one regarding the Sadom of Egypt. He saw the behavior of these other nations and he becomes a mirror of the disgust that God also feels for these nations, holding them in contempt. And in His contempt for those that oppose his people, Lazarus is very clear in sentence elven where God stands on this, *'And after three and a half days, The Living Spirit from God entered into them and they stood on their feet and The Spirit of Life fell upon them and great fear came over those who saw them.'* Though the world may celebrate what they view as a crushing defeat to Israel and call for the end of the Jewish nation, Israel and the Jewish people will rise up from this tragedy as if it was resurrected and it will retaliate with a force stronger than ever, so much so that the enemies of the Jews will be made to regret what they have done and they will fear for their own lives.

'And they heard a great voice from Heaven that said to them, "Come up here." And they went up to Heaven in a cloud and their enemies gazed at them.' What ensues is an endless wave of bombing and missile attacks by the Israeli Airforce that comes in such thick waves that they appear to be a dense cloud over their heads when the enemy looks up. At some point, the aggression of Israel's enemies will result in it attacking one of their major cities, of which Tehran comes to mind due to the constant threatening belligerence of the Ayatollahs to attack major cities in Israel. This is clearly indicated in the next sentence, *'And in that hour there was a great earthquake, and one out of ten cities fell, and the names of men who were killed in the earthquake were seven thousand, and the rest were in fear and gave glory to God who is in Heaven.'* Although the death of seven thousand would be minimal considering the population size of that city, the waves of bombs falling upon Tehran would result in at least ten percent of the city being damaged. Israel has already shown that they can attack Tehran without suffering any losses, but now that the air defenses of Iran have been destroyed, the city would be even more vulnerable than ever, At which point Lazarus hears the announcement that the second woe is concluded and that the third on will follow soon."

"But what about the rest of the chapter in Revelation," Pearce asked.

"What about it John. Take a good read of it and you will see that the next five lines appear to be completely unrelated to the remainder of this chapter. You have an angel telling everyone to rejoice that the worst is over. Either he is the dumbest angel in all of heaven being completely ignorant of the rest of the prophecy, because as we know the worst is yet to come, or these lines are merely an insertion by some Christian editor vainly attempting to restore some Christian content to the chapter as thus far it was clear that it was entirely about a restored Jewish nation and had nothing to do with Christianity. Take your pick John, which do you think it is?"

"Is there a third option?"

"Not that I'm aware of. This would be where I would suggest that Chapter Four of the restored document concludes. Those who stand with God, which happens to be a minority in today's world have now survived two of the woes. We see Israel taking the battle to the localized armies, militias, and terrorist groups that surround them, and from early appearances, one might mistakenly presume that they soundly defeated them. But this is the Middle East where common sense and logic has never prevailed. This is a region where a world has constantly waged war over a narrow coastal strip of land from which civilizations, cultures and religions have been birthed entirely out of proportion with its size or significance. And whatever one assumes to know about this region, they quickly come to the realization that they know absolutely nothing. God instructed Saul to kill every man, woman, child, and beast of the Amalekites and accept no ransom for their lives, but in his mercy, Saul decided to spare them from the total eradication, ultimately leading to his demise and loss of his kingdom to David. That's where the mistake began and the world, especially Israel has suffered for it repeatedly. Lazarus's vision will show us how little we've learned from this classic story in the Torah. The prophecy that Lazarus took from the Angel was definitely a bitter pill to swallow and no amount of honey to follow would ever remove the sourness from the belly of mankind. You know that we are not far away from the time of the events being revealed in this prophecy. You can see it on every news channel, in the words of our politicians, where no one is willing to speak the truth about current events. There is a crushing tide about to rise and unless we are willing to believe the prophecy, we will not be prepared for it. Woe to us, we are not prepared and therefore we cannot stop it!"

"You really believe that Doc? I thought you said we could change the course of events if we make an effort now."

"I would like to believe that we will come to realize that there is vile and rabid delirium that has possesses the minds of these anti-Zionist, anti-Israel and anti-Semitic mobs that spew their hatred constantly without any consequence and that will change at some point, and they will be held accountable. A Trump administration may be able to accomplish that. But what about after Trump. Will there be someone that will continue to condemn such abhorrent behavior or will everything simply return to the way it was? I still want to believe that a moral and just society can prevail. That all religions can remove the hatred from that which separates us and in turn we can celebrate together the common good and faith in God that unites us."

"So, you don't think it's possible then, Doc." Pearce saw right through my wishful thinking.

"Yeah, it's going to be tough."

CHAPTER TWELVE: BEAUTY AND THE BEAST

"I identify what is written in the next few chapters of Revelation as the fifth segment or chapter of what would have been the original book. What makes what I call chapter five distinct is the savagery of the imagery. In fact, the images that Lazarus was able to generate have been used over the past two millennia as the stories from which we spawn nightmares. The intensity and horror of the stories increases to such a degree from what he had described previously that not only has it has been used to terrify the people but now provides the framework of the demonic world that is a key component of Christianity. What was simply intended to be metaphors instead has become so literal that preachers and priests were able to convince their congregations to believe not only in evil magic but that there is this completely alternative dimension in which the Devil reigns supreme and it is his ultimate goal to bring the horrors of his own domain into our own."

"But you claimed that you don't believe any of that exists," Pearce was still surprised by my failure to accept the existence of Hell.

"Not in the least. Now that doesn't mean I don't believe that there aren't spiritual beings that God created that aren't happy with the fact that he also created mankind. I do believe there is some truth behind the story of Genesis 6 and from Job, we know that there is a Jewish concept of Satan as a troublemaker and a constant thorn in God's side. But having an animosity to mankind doesn't automatically make you the Evil King of the Dark Realm."

"What if you end up in Hell then Doc, once this life is all over? What will you say then?"

"I'd probably say, 'damn it! Peace was right.' But I won't need to because I know that's not going to happen.

"How can you be so certain."

"Because the God I believe in wouldn't create such a place," I insisted. "To create evil, one must be evil. One must know evil in order to imagine it and mold it into reality." I explained my take on the matter.

"True, but if God extended free will to Satan, then it would be the Devil creating these horrors and not God."

"I have two issues with that conclusion. One is that angels, even arch angels don't have the ability to create matter from energy. That is the sole privilege of God. Only He possesses that unique ability of creation. To say otherwise implies that there is more than one God, and I cannot accept that. Secondly, the Lord that I believe in, is omnipotent and all-seeing. Even if there was a dark angel that could create a Hell-like dimension, God would have been aware of it and would not have permitted such an event to occur. Once again, the Book of Job teaches us that Hell is something that can be manufactured during our own lifetimes, right here on Earth. I can assure you there are many people that will swear to you that every day they are living in Hell. There was even a time when I would wake up in the morning and say to myself, 'Oh crap, I'm still alive,' because I thought my life was such a living hell that I wanted to die. I got through it but there are thousands of perhaps even millions of people that don't. Try telling them that they're not in Hell and there's something worse out there that might be waiting for them. So, yes, I'm pretty certain that Lazarus was speaking metaphorically and there's not going to be any legions of demons, or a zombie apocalypse overrunning our world."

"I wish I could believe that" Pearce sighed, "But the Church has had to deal with too many exorcisms for me to doubt there isn't a Hell and our denying it is exactly what Satan would want us to do, in order to set a trap for us."

"I doubt I will be able to dissuade you, but I can assure you there is a simple meaning to Revelation chapter twelve and what follows."

"Have you ever questioned why it is that you believe you can decipher Revelation, whereas over the last two thousand years the most expert and knowledgeable theologians have struggled to do so? Don't you think you might be giving yourself too much credit Doc? How can you be so certain that you are right?"

"I thought you would have figured that out about me by now, John." Truthfully, I was actually surprised when he asked that question. You already know that I see a lot of things that others don't. That's been our entire history together."

'Yeah Doc, but that has to do with genetic memory, this thing you called GLEEM. It never had anything to do with prophecy."

"I think it's all part and parcel of the same thing. Being from a High Priestly family would suggest that we had a gift of prophecy, and I think along with the memories, that particular gift gets passed on genetically as well."

"So, why don't you give me an example Doc." Pearce was always the skeptic.

"I'll tell you about something I saw recently. My wife and I were sitting around this swimming pool. A typical rectangular pool, like you would see at any public pool, except this one was empty of water. There were quite a large number of people sitting at the edge of the pool but for some inexplicable reason, there were a few people standing in the deep end, but as I told you, it was dry. As I looked around, the people would randomly transform into a variety of animals. Cats, dogs, sheep, calves, ponies, and after a while they would change back again into their human form. It all seemed pretty harmless until one of the people standing in the deep end transitioned into a tiger. Before anyone could react, it snatched one of the small animals that was also present in the deep end and began to devour it. As long as everyone was in human form, they knew to stay away from the deep end, but they were unable to tear themselves from the pool and felt compelled to stay. As soon as they took on an animal form again, for whatever reason, they would jump back into the pool. The tiger would charge after them and most would manage to escape but, on some occasions, they weren't so lucky and were killed by the tiger. I can't explain why, but the tiger couldn't jump out of the pool. My wife suddenly transformed into a young doe and without hesitation jumped into the deep end. Fortunately, a deer can jump much higher than a tiger and she was able to leap out of the pool as soon as the tiger attempted to pounce. Once back safely on the side of the pool she became human again. I knew we should leave but we couldn't. We were bound to the place and stayed for what seemed like days. As might be expected, at some point my wife turned into the doe once again and leaped back into the pool. This time the tiger was waiting for her and it was on top of her before she could leap away. I picked up a wooden club, or it may have been a broken leg off one of the deck chairs, and jumped into the pool, beating the tiger senseless until he let her go. But it was too late, as I picked up the deer in my arms and it changed back into my wife, she exhaled her last breath."

"You said that was a prophecy," Pearce commented. "Seems to me that it is more likely a wild dream."

"It was definitely not a dream!"

"So, what do you think it means then?"

"My wife's parents became ill, both at the same time. Neither was ill enough to be booked into the hospital as in-patients, so they had to return each day for treatment as outpatients. Of course, that meant my wife would have to take them to the hospital each day for treatment, entering into the triage center where every known disease to mankind lay in waiting. I didn't accompany her on these visits, so it was only herself that was at risk. It wasn't long until she caught some sort of virus and it's already two week later and she's still suffering from its effects."

"Is she gravely ill," Pearce sounded concerned.

"No, not this time. I interpret this as the first jump into the deep end but no sooner did she tell me that she was ill, I insisted on her taking precautions."

"Such as?"

"Such as always wearing a mask whenever she goes back to the hospital. And having alcohol wipes readily available as soon as she makes contact with any object in the hospital.

"And that's working."

"Thus far she hasn't had to face a second tiger attack."

"You're convinced that was a prophecy about your wife."

"Well, it certainly wasn't about your wife," I replied sarcastically. If it wasn't an insight into what could possibly happen, then what was it? Let me tick off the boxes...did I see this happening at some time in the future? Yes. Was I awake when I viewed this imagery? As I told you, I believe so."

"You don't know if you were awake?" Pearce couldn't help but ask the obvious question.

"I wasn't sleeping, if that's what you want to know? I know that for certain. Best description would be that I was in a trance. I wasn't asleep but I still felt separated from the reality of the world. The same feeling you get when you're watching a movie, and you aren't aware of anything else happening in the room.

"Yeah, I know that feeling," Pearce confirmed he knew what I was talking about.

"But that's why I also know that a prophecy is only saying what may happen and not necessarily what will happen. There is an opportunity to change the future. As long as my wife stays away from hot spots in the hospital and wears a mask, I doubt my vision will be fulfilled. That holds true for every prophecy, or so I believe. But in order to stop it, then it is necessary that everyone understands it. You can only stop it if you know what to look for. That's why it is so important that everyone understands what the message in Revelations is."

"That would mean that we all have to interpret it the same way."

"Exactly. No use if we all have different opinions. We wouldn't even know where or when to start if we all had different interpretations. And Chapter 12 in Revelation certainly has generated a lot of opinions, especially concerning the woman that wears the sun as a cloak. You already know that your Catholic Church as well as the Eastern Orthodox Church teaches you that it is Mary, the mother of Jesus. The Protestants see the woman as symbolizing the church in general. There are even some groups that see her as representing Eve and view the dragon as her eternal battle with the snake from the Garden of Eden."

"But I'm assuming you disagree with all of those opinions."

"Of course I do. It is pretty clear who the woman is but in admitting so, all your religious leaders would need to admit that God's first love is still the Children of Israel. That would be a hard pill for them to swallow. Especially since the monks editing the book went to such great lengths to try and disguise the fact but if you read it closely, you'll see that their insertions are all out of context with the main storyline. In some places the grammatical structure is so awkward that you question whether the editors could speak any language at all,. But once all those additions are removed, it serves to clarify and enhance the content of what was originally authored by Lazarus. The beasts envisioned by him were symbolic, the numbers used to describe them significant, and even Christian scholars now recognize that the messages in Revelation were secret codes that were never intended to be interpreted literally. Just look at the first two sentences, '*And a great sign appeared in Heaven: a woman who was wearing the Sun, and the Moon was under her feet, and a crown of twelve stars on her head. And she was pregnant, and she cried out and was in labor; she was also in anguish to give birth.*' What you have here is virtually the same representation of God's bride as described by Isaiah. She is cloaked and protected in God's supreme light. It was always God's intention that we, as his people, would give birth to a better world, or as He described us, oir ha'oylum, a light unto the world. Lazarus lived at a time when astrology was still considered to be a science. The sun was synonymous with the ruling planet of Leo, which also represented the lion of Judah. The moon in astrology is seen as the huntress, almost always alone and isolated from the rest of the heavens. Or in this case, we envision Israel, shunned by the rest of the world, hated and despised beyond any sane reasoning. The twelve stars represent the twelve tribes of Israel, which are the nation's crowning glory. This imagery also aligns with Joseph's dream in Genesis 37:9-11, where he sees the sun, moon, and eleven stars bowing to him, representing Jacob also known as Israel, Rachel, and the twelve tribes of Israel. But also, throughout the Old Testament, Israel is depicted as the wife or bride of God as in Isaiah 54:5-6, Jeremiah 3:14 or Hosea 2:19-20. It was common long before and even in Lazarus's time to use marital imagery to describe God's covenant relationship with Israel. This symbolic imagery underscores Israel's role as a spiritual "bride" of God. There really is no other way in which the woman of his vison could be interpreted, but you can understand why the Church would be so hesitant to admit that God only has one true love, to which he is wed, and that is the nation of Israel."

"But what about the child she is going to give birth to," Pearce interrupted. "Clearly that is an indication of Jesus."

"And why would you think that?" I responded. "Jesus had already been born, lived and died already. The child in this prophecy hasn't even been born into this universe yet. The imagery, Old Testament references, and prophetic context all support a single interpretation, which emphasizes Israel's pivotal role in God's redemptive plan and His ongoing covenant relationship with His people. This unborn child aligns with that narrative and therefore is the future messiah that will redeem the Jews and fulfil God's promise to them. Look what Lazarus writes next, '*And another sign appeared in Heaven and behold, a great fiery Dragon that has seven heads and ten horns, and upon its heads seven diadems. And its tail dragged the third of the stars that are in the Heavens and cast them upon The Earth; and the Dragon was standing before the woman who was ready to give birth, that when she had delivered, it would devour her child.*' He's managed to describe in a single image the entire history of the Jewish people not only up to his time but well beyond it so that it even includes our present time. It represents the evil that Israel had to face thus far, each enemy wishing to destroy them, but also the greatest enemy that is yet to come that will attempt to devour the entire Jewish race and eliminate them forever. Seven distinct times that were devoted to Israel's destruction since the dawn of my people. Assyria, Babylon, Persia, Greece, Rome, the Holy Roman pan-European Empire with its inquisitions, Nazi Germany, and now we can expect the seventh; the most threatening of all. But this last threat is greater than all the rest, as witnessed by the dragon's tail dragging a third of the stars behind it and casting them into the battle. If Israel is only represented by the twelve stars in the woman's crown, then the stars being cast by the dragon must represent a third of the world's population. This would suggest that the final evil empire can draw on a massive population of well over two billion people. An interesting number since according to the last decade's statistics on the world population said there were 2.08 billion Muslims at that time. As you can see, the numbers selected by Lazarus were not random. Even though there was no such thing as a Muslim entity in his time, he was able to foresee the future existence of their total population as represented by the stars. He was not suggesting that all two billion would participate in the final battle, but only that there was that number present on the earth at the particular time of the End of Days, so that based upon the number we would be able to know that this the time. Sentence six provides us with another detail that demonstrates the woman must be Israel. She flees into the wilderness, much in the same way that the Jews fled into the desert after their

Exodus from Egypt. For twelve hundred and sixty days, she hides in the desert, that same magic number that Lazarus has mentioned repeatedly when describing the temple earlier. Which raises the question as to why he is constantly raising this number as the time frame for his predictions. Because it connects to the times mentioned in Daniel 7:25 and 12:7."

"And now I suspect that you want me to remember what was written in Daniel, just like that," Pearce seemingly expected that I would want him to know every verse in the Bible.

"No, I don't. That is why I will tell you what it says in Daniel. Verse 7:25, is a reference to the beast with ten horns that takes over the world for a period of a time, a times and a half time. Verse 12:7 says that the breaking or slaughter of the holy people being Israel shall take place a time, a times and a half time."

"I don't see the connection," he complained.

"It's all in the way we look at the numbers. We can say 1260 days, or we could also say three and a half years. Though Daniel is not as specific, he does say a time, which could be one year, plus a times, which could be two times or two years, and a half time which would be half a year. All together that would be three and a half years."

"In that case, you're saying that Jochanan or Lazarus was even more specific than Daniel was, even though they may have been seeing the same prophecy."

"That is a possibility," I agreed. "Though we still don't know if a day of prophecy is actually a day of real time. What both were trying to say is that there is a plan. God has runs everything according to a set schedule. And if the final battle is only three and a half years, then we can probably survive that. But if it should be three and a half decades, the suffering during and afterwards will be immeasurable. Now as I told you earlier, the Church editors inserted their additions in a manner which appears to be totally out of context with the events of the story. Sentences ten through twelve are what I'm speaking of. In sentence nine the dragon is cast down to earth, where we see in sentence thirteen, he continues to wreak havoc. Nine is connected directly to thirteen. Whereas ten to twelve have Jesus and his supporters in heaven rejoicing from out of nowhere. Hardly a time to rejoice as we can see from what follows is the continuous persecution of the woman representing Israel, yet here are these sentences obviously inserted but definitely in the wrong place."

"I'm still confused about this number's thing. You just seem to have pulled this rule of a time, a times and a half to mean one, two time, and a half, out of thin air."

"It might appear that way, but Lazarus gave the key to his numbers and those in Daniel in sentence fourteen of this chapter. *'And to the woman were given two wings of a great eagle, that she might fly into the wilderness, into her place, where she is nourished for a time, and times, and half a time, from the face of the serpent.'* He uses Daniel's exact wording to describe his own time period of three and a half years. Therefore, there can be no doubt that he and Daniel are using the same formula. But as I was trying to say, from the last sentence of the chapter, the war was far from over, and any rejoicing with Jesus as the editors attempted through their inserted three sentences was clearly premature. The same way they made an addition to the last sentence which is obviously not grammatically correct as they attempted to insert Jesus once again into a sentence where he didn't belong. *'And the dragon was wroth with the woman, and went to make war with the remnant of her seed, which keep the commandments of God,'* That is how the sentence should have read in its entirety, indicating that although she had given birth to the Messiah, he was not yet of an age to fight in the battle, so the dragon took advantage of going against the rest of her children, meaning the children of Israel without the Messiah to lead them."

"But couldn't that last sentence have meant that not only did the dragon go to war against the children of Israel, referenced as the remnant of her seed, but also against the Christians if you were to keep the rest of the sentence from my version of the text which said, *'those that kept the testimony of Jesus Christ.'* I would think that would make sense."

"You might have a good point if it wasn't for what was written in the next chapter," I advised. "Chapter thirteen indicates that hardly anyone kept the testimony of Jesus after the beast takes control. That becomes obvious in sentence eight of that chapter where the same editors inserted the phrase *'of the lamb'* after the book of life. No where in your Christian teaching is there a reference to Jesus having a book of life. The Book of Life is a concept exclusive to Judaism, representing a divine record in which the names of the righteous from the beginning of time have been inscribed. It symbolizes God's remembrance of those who lead virtuous lives, ensuring their eternal life or blessings in the world to come. This concept is reinforced during the High Holy Days of Rosh Hashanah and Yom Kippur, when the Jews pray to be inscribed in the Book of Life for the coming year. The original concept of the book stems from Exodus 32:32-33 in which following the sin of the Golden Calf, Moses pleads with God to forgive the Israelites, saying, *'But now, if You will forgive their sin, fine; but if not, erase me from the book You have written.'* And to which God responds, *'Whoever has sinned against Me, I will erase from My book.'* We can also find a reference to the book in Psalm 69:28, which is a request to punish the enemies of the Jewish people saying, *'May they be blotted out of the book of life, and may they not be recorded with the righteous.'* Furthermore, regarding the End of Days, in Daniel 12:1 it is written, *'At that time your people shall be delivered, everyone who is found written in the book.'* As you can see, these passages suggest the existence of a heavenly ledger where the fate of individuals is recorded, reflecting their righteousness or sinfulness. At no point is this book ever attributed to Jesus, but the editors made a desperate attempt to do so. Most likely the wording was the Book of Life of those slain from the foundation of the world and with the quick strokes of a feathered pen, 'of those' became 'of the Lamb.'

Time for another break because I desperately need a coffee. We'll continue with the battle as described in chapter thirteen because the war is far from over. But you know my policy, no coffee, no work!"

"I've heard that you say that every time you're working at a site in China."

"I guess it's become a bit of a meme wherever I go now. As soon as I sit down in one of their offices for a meeting they look at me and say 'bu kafe, bu gongzoa.' It actually surprises me that they know that even when it is the first time we're meeting. I can only assume someone is spreading the word throughout the industry."

"Guess you're famous in China for that phrase now," Peace laughed.

"Part of my legacy," I laughed in return.

CHAPTER THIRTEEN: SIGNS OF THE BEAST

"I have a question," Pearce didn't even wait until I finished my second cup of coffee.

"Alright, fire away."

"In the last chapter it says in sentence five that the man-child delivered by the woman would rule the nations with a rod of iron. Why iron?"

"In the Aramaic version it says to shepherd the nations with a rod of iron, but rule or shepherd doesn't matter as it implies the same thing. Unlike your Messiah, Jesus, who said to beat swords into plough shares, and generally seemed to be against violence, this Messiah doesn't hold a scepter of gold or silver but one of iron, the metal from which all weapons of war were forged. He was born in strife, into a world of conflict and his existence, as he finally assumes the throne of mankind will be filled with the stench of blood from the moment he takes on the mantle of leadership. I'd like to believe this war only lasts three and a half years, but I don't think so. As I explained before, a year on God's calendar could just as easily be a decade or even a generation. That wasn't the question I thought you were going to ask."

"What did you think I would ask?" Pearce was curious.

"I thought you would ask why the dragon and the beast coming out of the sea are described in almost the same way?"

"Well, I was going to ask that next," he quipped.

"Because the dragon and the beast aren't to be taken literally as Satan or demonic creatures. They represent the same thing and that is why it says the beast has derived all of its power and authority from the dragon because they are one and the same. The imagery of the seven heads and ten horns is drawn directly from Daniel chapter seven. It symbolizes he oppressive kingdoms and rulers that have plagued the Jews over their entire existence. On a more spiritual level, the parallel descriptions emphasize the pervasive and systemic nature of evil. The dragon as Satan operates both in the spiritual realm, but on our plane of existence the beast operates through political or societal systems. Together they show that opposition to God and his chosen people spans both realms. Just as it says, '*And I stood on the sand of the Sea, and I saw a beast ascending from the Sea, which had ten horns and seven heads, and upon its horns, ten diadems, and upon its heads the name of blasphemy. And The Beast that I saw was like a leopard, and its feet like those of a wolf and its mouth like that of lions, and the Dragon gave its throne, its power and great authority to it.*' The power base of this beast is symbolized by the leopard, the wolf and the lion, the same three animals that played a significant role in Dante's Inferno, and to which scholars of that literature, including my third-great grandfather, Jakob, who translated Dante's work into Hebrew, spent copious amounts of time attempting to decipher the meaning of the animals but without any certainty. Sometimes the metaphor of Dante's dark woods and the creatures that live within it cannot be seen for the forest from the trees. We know the leopard can't change its spots, the she-wolf is insatiable, always hungering for more, and the lion is the king of the jungle, and therefore it is a matter of equating which nations could match this description within our own time. There happens to be two emerging powers in our world at this time that can easily match the animals mentioned. Neither can change their spots no matter how hard they try. The Russian Federation is still the same beast that once crushed opposition as the Soviet Union. It hungers to expand its dominion, but it lacks the economic power to be king of the jungle, and the lack of manufacturing finished products would suggest it can't attain that position. Whereas China has established itself as the major economic power in our world, having investments on a global scale, bank rolling nations to such a degree that they hold their debts and assets. Napoleon once warned the other nations to not disturb the dragon's sleep because once it awakes it will control the world. Two hundred years later that warning is now a reality. The world does not marvel after Russia, but it does pander and feed the ravenous appetite of the Chinese international economy."

"If I'm not mistaken," Pearce was about to raise an objection again, "I was taught it had the feet of a bear. It was leopard, bear and lion."

"Once again it depends on which version you're reading. My version which precedes the King James version by fifteen hundred years says wolf. So, I'm going with wolf."

"Guess it doesn't make a difference. Just surprised how much it can change."

"You shouldn't be. I've already told you that the Chrisian editors were busy. But continuing on, as we know, the beast is a composite. So, it does not necessarily mean it is all one nation we can point to. But instead, it is many nations that have formed an alliance. But they all have one thing in common. That's blasphemy. It is written on all the heads of the beast."

"How should we define blasphemy?" Pearce asked.

"I believe the basic definition is that blasphemy refers to showing disrespect, irreverence, or contempt for God, sacred things, or religious beliefs. In a modern context, blasphemy can extend beyond religious frameworks to include any expression that deeply offends religious sensibilities. That would mean that any time I suggest to you that Jesus was not the son of God, you could accuse me of blaspheming or offending your religious sensibility. But then I could say the same to you, any time you imply that the Jews are no longer God's chosen people. So, I think we have to elevate the actual meaning to imply we must actually denigrate or desecrate, the religious practice or objects of another's beliefs."

"As in attacking another religion's place of worship. Is that what you mean?"

"That and generally just preventing the overt practice of one's religion. Committing violence against a person or property simply because they practice a different religion, or any religion as may be the case."

"That certainly narrows it down."

"It certainly does," I agreed. "You're looking at either a government that prohibits religious practices in public or a religion which condemns any other practice but its own and is willing to commit violence against members of those other religions."

"And it's obvious whom you have in mind," Pearce knew exactly what I was saying.

"I think it is pretty easy to determine who the beast is representing. The third and fourth sentences agree with me. *'And one of its heads was as if it had been crushed to death and its mortal wound was healed, and all The Earth marveled after The Beast. And they worshiped the Dragon that gives authority to The Beast, and they worshiped The Beast saying, "Who is like this Beast, and who is able to war with it?"'* Just have to look at past empires that were once dominant in this world that lost all their authority only to gain it back in our time. These talking heads have the gift of twisting words, incite hatred, but more importantly they can deceive the leaders of the free world into doing their bidding.

"I admit, I can't determine which empire the is represented by the head that was wounded practically to the point of death."

"One might guess the reference is to the Ottoman Empire, but that never really died. Just became partitioned into a number of Arab states that are a threat but not unified enough to be considered healed and filling the world with awe. China, well that was a great empire in its own mind. Yes, it has become a major power under its communist regime, but it never suffered what could be considered a deadly wound. Now the Soviet Union, which was an empire that died and for a few years after 1989, the world considered it to be dead and buried. There was an expectation that somehow it would be controlled by the west, and it would never be a threat again. Well, it has risen like a phoenix from the ashes, and it may not be the Soviet Union, but the Russian Federation has all its weaponry and manpower available once again. The rest of the world may have thought that could never happen, but it did, and the world definitely wonders how it accomplished this feat and how it keeps getting stronger with each passing day. This capacity to continually grow in power and gain dominance refers to the beast in its entirety. Through its coalition partners, it has become a military and economic powerhouse that rivals the western nations. The BRICS alliance has even brought together nations that one would never have imagined could sit at a table together. Just like it says in sentence seven that *'power was given him over all kindreds, and tongues and nations.'* We could expect an alliance between kindred spirits such as China, Russian, North Korea and Iran, but how is it that India, South Africa, Algeria, Belarus, Bolivia, Cuba, Indonesia, Kazakhstan, Malaysia, Nigeria, Thailand, Turkey, Uganda, Uzbekistan, Viet Nam, thee United Arab Emirates, Ethiopia and Egypt all belong to it now?"

"I didn't realize they had expanded to that degree," Pearce admitted he hadn't kept up with the news. "Some of those countries are allied to the western nations. Turkey is even part of Nato."

"I already told you that the prophecy has warned us about trusting Turkey. It doesn't surprise me at all that is throwing its hat in with China, Russia and Iran. But our media has kept this all low key. They don't want us to see that there has been a tremendous shift in power. Even those we thought of as allies will place their allegiance with our enemies because in this new beast, they see an opportunity to achieve all of their goals, even if that means dealing through deception, and we apparently are falling for it, just as the prophecy says we will. You will see, more and more nations will hand over authority to this emerging power. Some for profit, others because they naively believe it will lead to peace. We will delude ourselves into thinking that the skirmishes that continue to break out all over the world will eventually come to an end, without considering that the death toll continues to mount even as we are promised peace is at hand."

"You're suggesting that even if we manage to sign peace treaties, it's merely an illusion."

"Perhaps more correctly stated, it is a delusion," I confirmed. "Peace only serves as a cover for their true intentions. Our desire for peace is a weakness and they know how to exploit it. But there is still an element of distrust among enough people that we don't blindly surrender everything to them. They're aware of this last wall of resistance and they formulate a plan as to how they can eliminate it. It's all made clear in sentence eleven onwards, *'And I saw another Beast that ascended from the ground, and it had two horns and was like a lamb but spoke like The Dragon. And it will exercise all the authority of the former Beast before it and will make The Earth and those living in it also to worship the first Beast, whose mortal wound was healed.'* I think it's pretty clear what happens. Do you see it as well?"

"I agree the world has gone a little crazy lately," Pearce provided his take on recent events. "In fact, it had spun out of control. But the election this November put Trump back in office and that is a deterrent to all the changes being made. If he gets tough with China and Iran again, that should end any likelihood that we all get in bed with our adversaries."

I shook my head. "You're presuming that America still controls the Westen hemisphere. I don't believe it does any more. They've already anticipated that America would swing to the right again and they've made their contingency plans to counteract that impact. That lamb that you've been taught is the Antichrist, isn't the Antichrist at all. It's the anti-American. It's their secret weapon to destroy any attempt of America interfering with their takeover."

"Now you're saying there's no such thing as the Antichrist," Pearce was obviously resistant to that notion. "Well, I disagree!"

"If I have made my case successfully that this is in reality a Jewish document, then it must be recognized that there was no inclusion by Lazarus of Jesus Christ at all. And if there was no Christ, then you can't possibly have any reference to an Antichrist. It's pretty clear that what Lazarus is trying to point out is that a wolf in sheep's clothing is going to be elevated into a position of supreme power somewhere in the Western world. The Jochanan that you want to believe wrote this book, would have perhaps seen Jesus as a lamb figure but the Lazarus I'm describing is reliant on the writings of the Old Testament prophets where they referred to the lamb. Jeremiah 11:19 says, *'I had been like a gentle lamb led to the slaughter; I did not realize that they had plotted against me, saying, "Let us destroy the tree and its fruit; let us cut him off from the land of the living, that his name be remembered no more."'* Jeremiah is comparing himself to a lamb, highlighting his innocence and the treachery of those who seek his life. His purpose is to underscores the vulnerability of the righteous in the face of evil. In this case, the good lambs get slaughtered, but the bad ones, as being described by Lazarus, they become as powerful as the dragon. The contrast is demonstrated dramatically in Isaiah 53:7. *'He was oppressed and afflicted, yet he did not open his mouth; he was led like a lamb to the slaughter, and as a sheep before its shearers is silent, so he did not open his mouth.'* Isaiah is referring to the suffering servant which is representing the Children of Israel. Over and over again we have been led to the slaughterhouse without saying a word. Some would like to say this is a reference to the suffering servant that is found in 52:13-15 but when you examine those lines closely, the subject of these verses is despised for having been deemed successful and worthy of God's attention, and this has only served to garner the hatred of other nations because they consider this servant to be unlike them, a miscreant and unworthy. A blemish on the world that must be destroyed. The lamb of God, a creature despised, hated, detested, scorned, unable to defend itself by its own imposed silence, whereas the lamb of the beast, is boisterous, worshipped, desired, honoured and followed by the nations of the world. Lazarus uses this comparison for two reasons. The first is to suggest that the people in our time would sooner trust and follow those they consider to be beautiful and having the gift of oration, than someone they consider homely and less glib with the tongue. The second reason has to do with pomp and ceremony. Lazarus infers that the people can be easily swayed by light shows and magic tricks, which this lamb-like beast is more than capable of providing."

"Simple language please Doc. I'm trying to follow you but you're making it difficult."

"I thought it was quite obvious," I was surprised that he couldn't grasp my point. "Bottom line is there's going to be this wolf in sheep's clothing that arises in one of the Western countries. I don't think it is America because of the political shift to the right that's happened there but it has to be a county that is seen as a superpower or at least semi-powerful. That narrows it down to Britain, France or Germany as the countries I believe most likely to throw in with the enemy. A leader will rise in that country with an extremely polished and developed gift of oratory, exuding charisma and charm, but add to this an extremely cunning and devious intelligence, which appears sincere as if it is fueled by integrity and honesty. He will be a great showman and even the people in America will beg to follow him. That's why I personally think it will be Britain. First of all, there won't be a language barrier, and I lived through the days when the Beatles first came onto the music world scene. Americans went absolutely crazy over the four British lads from Liverpool. The Yanks love Brits!"

"How do you know it's a he?" Pearce raised the diversity issue which has been ingrained into so many.

"I don't and I can't dismiss that possibility. My version of Revelation uses the word '*seduce*' in sentence fourteen, where I believe your later version uses the word '*deceiveth.*' Seduces implies there could be a sexual nature to why people hang on to this lamb's every word."

"Sort of like Taylor Swift," Pearce suggested.

"I personally could never understand why so many young people treat everything she says as if it's gospel. But yes, this person will have that same kind of power over the people. It's actually a good example, John, because it shows how easy it would be to gain the trust and worship of that particular generation of Americans. But more importantly, I look at what is written in sentence fifteen and I recognize how easy it is to spread a message of hate as well. '*And it was given to it to give spirit to the image of The Beast and to cause that all who would not worship the image of The Beast would be murdered.*' You only have to look at the college campuses and in the streets of those same cities and see how what many would consider as the more intelligent component of the population, being brainwashed into marching and chanting, "From the River to the Sea" and attacking every Jew and Israel supporter that crosses their path. Try to explain that they are chanting for the genocide of a people, while acting on the behest of an evil that represented nothing but sixty years of terror and murder and they look at you as if you're the one that is clueless. Yes, this world has already proven how easy it would be for an evil entity to take control. There's an entire generation just waiting to be led astray."

"What you are saying is that it is inevitable and the End of Days is unavoidable," Pearce concluded.

"I know it seems that way. If we do not commit to go to war to stop the beast, then they will still manage to continue their terror attacks on a global scale, and we will all be endangered as we watch our freedoms eventually slip away. But should we make the decision to go to war, then we are also placing our families and future at risk of Armageddon. Sort of a Catch-w22. That being the choice we have to make, I would rather bring the wrath of God down upon them at the time and place of my choosing, rather than be sitting and waiting for them to bring their brand of violence to my neighborhood. As Isaiah wrote, '*because of his silence the suffering servant was brought to the slaughter like a lamb*'. Therefore, we cannot choose to remain silent and inactive. I certainly can't remain silent any longer. The Book of Revelation reveals that we must take up the sword against this enemy but in doing so we have to appreciate that we may be engaging in a fight that lasts for generations before we can ever claim a victory and along the way both sides will suffer terribly. Many of our loved ones will be lost along the way."

"There's got to be another way," Pearce insisted. "What you are proposing is a no-win situation. If we don't fight, we lose, but if we do fight, we may win but we also lose. There has to be another option!"

"Be careful what you wish for. The most astounding inference in Revelation is that Lazarus recognizes that the coming war is one of ideology and that is why it will take a long time before the enemy is finally vanquished. And that also is what the American government and its people in general don't appreciate; no matter how the war begins, it is not that we are being attacked by several nations as much as by a concept, an unholy belief that is so pervasive, that one can kill without even thinking of it as murder. The enemy is convinced that what they are doing is a blessing and until we can understand this mindset, we will continually try to negotiate, to trade, to buy them off, thinking eventually they will abandon this ideology. It will never happen! Has Nazism disappeared? No. In fact it grows stronger every day as well with its pervasive argument for anti-Semitism taking place currently all over the world. Everything has turned so upside-down now that those of us opposed to anti-Semitism are now the ones accused of being Nazis. As the latest US government document reporting on hate crimes in their country revealed, over seventy percent of those crimes are being perpetrated currently against Jews. It doesn't matter that radical Muslims are killing innocent civilians in places like San Bernardino, or Paris, or a dozen other places around the world, the real enemy must be the Jews, no matter what the circumstances, and that is why it is nearly impossible to defeat an ideology. When you have reached a point where someone may be staring down the barrel of a gun and all they can say to their attacker is do me the favour of killing that Jew over there first before you kill me, then and only then will you recognize the danger we are facing. Lazarus saw it, and hopefully as I restore his book to its original Hebraic origin, you and many others will see it too. Many like yourself are still faced with the dilemma of believing this to be a Christian book, and therefore the case against anti-Semitism can't be relevant to your concerns. But you have to look past that and believe me! The redactions done by the Catholic scholars between the second and fourth centuries, by men such as Justyn Martyr, Ignatius, and especially Jerome only managed to create a book that you as a Christian have called Revelation, thinking it solely for believers in Christ and failing to see that it's message is far more universal. Strip away all their additions, which as I have shown you are easy to identify, due to the sudden differences in style and context, and you will find essentially what is the most prophetic Hebrew book ever written, with a message for everyone of a Judeo-Christian heritage and specifically pointing towards our present timeframe. And therefore, the most obvious warning of its message coming true at this time is the rising tide of anti-Semitism that is being fueled by radical Islam throughout the world. but most egregiously in the Western nations. As we approach the end of my efforts to restore the writing to its original content, with only two more chapters to go, you will see that the conclusion of Revelation is only the beginning of the catastrophe about to befall all of us."

CHAPTER FOURTEEN: MARK OF THE BEAST

'*And it will cause all, small and great, rich and poor, Masters and Servants, to be given a mark on their right hands or on their foreheads, that no one may buy or sell again except one who has on him the mark of the name of The Beast or the number of its name. Here is wisdom, and whoever has a mind in him, let him calculate the number of the beast, for it is the number of a man -- six hundred and sixty-six.*' "You can't get much more prophetic than that," I commented.

"Nothing new about that Doc," Pearce dismissed my comment as if the secret was known long ago. "All we need to do is look for the number 666 and we will know who our enemies are."

"Hate to disappoint you John, but by now you should have realized that nothing that Lazarus says is as simple as that. Any time he provides a number it is a code and unless you break the code you don't have any real idea what he is actually referring to. His statement that the number is a product of mankind is most illuminating. It can mean that it is a theoretical product of a specific civilization's creative endeavor, or it could be referring to a physical product that is actually manufactured by a particular civilization."

"If that's the case, then how can you possibly figure it out. Why can't it simply be a number?" he whined.

"Because if it was simply a number, he wouldn't have said that whoever has a mind in him, inferring having some intelligence or intellect out of the ordinary, then that person will be able to calculate or decipher the meaning of six hundred and sixty-six. He's already telling you that it is a clue but should not be taken as the final answer or at face value.

"So, it's not 666?"

"He was making a private little joke," I explained. He knew that the majority of people that read the book would not understand it and would simply accept it as a mark, like a tattoo, that they should look for. It's the number of man, he says, telling you right away that it is not some number manufactured by the beast. It is a device of mankind, which also should tell you that there is no beast, only the savagery of man."

"What's so funny that he'd consider it to be a joke."

"It's very funny. For almost two thousand years, Christian scholars have been looking into the realm of the fantastic, the mystical, and even the demonical in order to find an answer. All it's done is result in overwhelming interpolation, confusion and a series of horror movies where they suspect its use for political and self-gratifying motivation. Just think of all those Hollywood movies where the villain pulls back their hair and there behind their ear is the numbers 666 that existed as a birthmark from the time they were born. It's pretty funny when you think about it."

"Then what is it about?" Pearce once again asked impatiently. "If it's not a birthmark, then what do you think it is."

"It's a reference to certain keys that are the product of man. What you must appreciate, John, is this; Lazarus provided a number that he knew would have meaning from his time until the final days. It had to be a number that would reveal specific points about mankind's present and future. He didn't know exactly when the End of Days would come about but he knew until that time, there would be a series of hardships that would befall not only the Jews but also any of the true believers in God. He already saw that the suffering would exist throughout several epochs. As a Jew, Lazarus could write in Hebrew and Aramaic. He acknowledges in Revelations that he used both because he needed those that were close to him, those within his inner circle to read his prophecy and understand. He also knew that those outside his immediate circle would have difficulty translating and deciphering his meaning and he intended it to be so for his own personal protection. He had to be careful at who he may have been pointing a finger at, especially if the Romans thought he was proposing an insurrection against their rule."

"In other words, Doc, you're saying he never wrote 666."

"He couldn't," I stated emphatically. "Only our current civilization could be so callous and egocentric to think that the number he wrote would have been 666. What we call Arabic numerals weren't even invented in his time. They aren't even Arabic numerals. They were invented in India in the sixth century, passed on to the Arabs in the eight century and didn't reach Europe until the tenth century. That being the case, the mark of the Beast being 666 had only existed for approximately four hundred years before it got recorded in the King James version as such. You might say that prior to then he was a completely different beast and identified in a completely different manner."

"If that's the case, then what did he write?"

"Lazarus provides the first key by saying he wrote in Hebrew and Aramaic for his immediate circle. That being the case, then he wrote the number as תרס"ו as Hebrew uses letters to represent numbers. As such, the number also spells out a word, Tarsu which was a city in Anatolia as the Jews would have called it, or Tarsus as it was known in the Roman world, much in the same way that the name Jeshua becomes Jesus."

"Why would he suggest the number of the beast was the city of Tarsus?" Pearce was bewildered by that tidbit of information.

"Because he considered the man from Tarsus as the greatest threat to what he was teaching to his Minean followers. Saul of Tarsus, or Paul, proclaimed himself to be a Jew, and that all his followers should be considered Jews, and thus the inheritors of the promise to the Jews, but at the same time his teachings strayed as far as possible from Judaism. As far as Jochanan or Lazarus was concerned, in his time period, the followers of Paul were the enemy. Remember, Lazarus was bearing witness to the lasting effects of a man who was not a true apostle but proclaimed that he, himself was to be considered as no less than any of the superlative apostles who had actually known Jesus. As more and more converts followed the teachings of Paul, Lazarus recognized that the followers of the original teachings of the Jerusalem Church were threatened and as a result of the eventual fall of the Jerusalem Church he had to escape to Ephesus for his own protection. Yes, he was a hunted man by the Roman authorities, but also by the new Christians that saw him as a heretic for adhering to the original Chrisian religious beliefs and not those preached by Paul."

"But wouldn't that mean that the Beast was limited to his time?"

"Not if that number could be used as a key to unlock several prophecies simultaneously," I tried to make him understand the uniqueness of this number and why it was selected by Lazarus.

"I don't understand how a single prophecy can apply to several different interpretations. That doesn't sound like a prophecy at all. More like multiple choice in order to make it fit whatever conclusion one wants to believe."

"You'll understand once I explain the other keys to you. Lazarus wanted his followers to understand that the Beast always exists. It's present throughout time and has as its sole purpose the destruction of the Children of Israel. If he could present a number that could be applied to multiple time periods and still be accurate in his depiction, then you have to admit that would be pretty amazing. A number that could be universally applied. That would have to be unique. Wouldn't' you agree?"

"Yes, I guess so. If that was possible."

"More than possible. In fact, it was genius. So, he writes the number in Hebrew, but he knows at some point the book is going to be translated into Latin and distributed through the Roman world. So, the number has to be significant to any of his followers that can only speak Latin, and this is where the second key becomes even more obvious. Once again, I remind you that the revelation of the beast must extend throughout time. He knew the Roman Empire would persist for centuries still to come because there was no other rising empire strong enough to challenge it. The Empire would write its numbers out in Roman numerals, and therefore six hundred and sixty-six would be written as DCLXVI, which is a very unique number in all of the Roman counting system. It is the only number which uses all of the common Roman numerals, only once and in their proper descending order. The number for a thousand or M was rarely used and was often simply an implied number, similar to the lack of an actual thousandth letter in Hebrew. Therefore, the uniqueness of this number as written in Roman numerals is a clear indication that he wished us to recognize that the Empire existed as the Beast too. It's ordered, regimented systems; even its attempt to conquer the world in order brink all of mankind under its yoke, is symbolized by this uniquely structured number. Not to mention one of the prime reasons for his hiding in exile was the fact that he was a wanted man by Roman justice. Lazarus had no knowledge of when the Roman Empire would end but he presumed even if it was eventually replaced, that throughout future history, the oppression of the Jews and the Gentile obsession and commitment to destroy Israel would not abate. Therefore, the number 666 in Roman numerals would remain significant in designating the beast for a long time, even after the disappearance of Rome as the center of the world. Pretty amazing that one number could be so unique that it could reflect different histories as well as the future."

"That's it?" Pearce didn't seem all that impressed.

"No! There's a third key. If we agree that Lazarus was a normal person, then he'd have absolutely no clue as to what would happen in the period 660 to 666 AD. But if his prophecy did ring true, then he would at least know that year would be significant in regard to the rising of the Beast though he may not know exactly how. Does that sound like a reasonable presumption?"

"I can technically agree with that," Pearce nodded.

"The reason I said a range between 660 and 666 AD is because of the error in dating the birth of Jesus. If we were looking to be the most accurate, then knowing that Jesus was born between 5 or 6 BC as we already discussed, then six hundred and sixty-six years later would be the year 660 AD but if we continue to go with the standard dating, then it would be 666 AD. Either way, Prior to 660, the birth of Islam had been off to a pretty rocky start. Internally they had been fighting what was called the First Fitna, or civil war. Mohammed had died twenty-four years earlier and the leaders were now assassinating one another at a hectic pace. Abu Bakr, the first Caliph was dead two years after Mohammed and nominated Umar to succeed him on his death bed. Umar did last as second caliph for ten years before being assassinated in 654. Uthman, the third Caliph was assassinated in 656 and Ali ibn Abi Talib became the fourth caliph only to be assassinated in 661. Muawiya then declares himself caliph and by 666 AD he's eliminated most of his enemies and his Umayyad dynasty begins, finally bringing about some semblance of stability to the struggling religion known as Islam. And once stabilized, that's when Islam was able to secure the expansion of its empire. The Islamic empire was now in a phase of consolidation and expansion. The military campaigns against the Byzantine Empire were successful in that they were able to push deeper into Anatolia. Their forces were able to advance further along North Africa into what is now Tunisia and Algeria. A system of provincial governors was established with allegiance to the capital in Damascus. Muawiya began building a naval fleet to challenge Byzantine control of the Mediterranean, and both road networks and communication systems were improved to facilitate trade and commerce. What should have died early in its infancy with one leader assassinating another, by the year 666 AD after defying the odds against its success, had become a powerful threat to the rest of the world and continues to be one, as long as there are Islamic extremists permitted to run unopposed because bleeding heart liberals consider it racist if we focus on their criminality. But as for 666 AD, it was the year that changed the world. And right now, that third key to the number of the beast might be the most dangerous prediction of them all."

"So, in your opinion that third key is the true number of the Beast?"

"You're missing the point, John. They're all the number of the Beast. They're all true! Lazarus was able to seize upon a singular number that applied to multiple predictions of the most traumatic threats that Judaism had to face. The first key was the creation of an offshoot of Judaism that didn't see itself any longer as a sect of Judaism but was destined to become an antagonist as it fostered a child that demanded its parent's inheritance. The second key was a ruthless military empire that caused the single greatest dispersion of Jews across the globe, minimizing the Jewish presence in its own homeland and even forbidding Jews to refer to their country by its proper name and refusing to let them pray upon their own temple mount under the punishment of death. Jews were forced to call themselves Palestinians, a name that Hadrian selected from our rich history of arch enemies, the Philistines. How degrading, to force a proud race with a history of over a thousand years at that time to call themselves after the name of a despised ancient enemy. And now that name continues to haunt us even to the present day. The third key was the establishment of a religious theocracy that calls for the death and slaughter of Jews one hundred and nineteen times in their Quran. And once again, that same threat exists today and has not diminished. But what I haven't told you about yet is the fourth key. And that key does apply directly to our time. In this case the key is not so much a number as a symbol. It's a symbol we've seen thousands of times in our everyday lives. I need you to close your eyes and picture the belly of the sixes overlapping, their stems pointing to nine o'clock, one o'clock, and five o'clock. Now rotate those sixes for two hours and let the stems leave a trail. Can you see it?"

"It's the symbol for radioactivity," Pearce exclaimed somewhat surprised as he kept his eyes closed.

"Now you will see the Beast in its most terrible form of all. Remember I told you that Lazarus was saying the number could represent both a theoretical and a physical product of civilization. Well, here's your physical product and it's the most terrifying key of all. Man's ability to harness the power to obliterate civilization as we know it. But you can also find these same three sixes buried in the design for biohazardous substances and what is known as the Trilateral Organization."

"Never heard of them," Pearce was quick to respond.

"It's a group of world elitists, including banking organizations that was founded in 1973 by David Rockefeller. Considering its members include political leaders, business executives, and intellectuals from North America, Europe and Japan, you might be excused if you begin to think their main purpose is to dominate the world economy. Apparently they meet regularly but exactly what their goal is does not appear to be public knowledge. You and I will never get a formal invitation to attend one of their meetings. Since the group claims to have no formal governmental or executive powers, then what possibly could be its purpose. How interesting that they too designed their logo on the same basic structure of three interlocking sixes, as can be seen for both radiation and biological hazards. Coincidence? Trust me John, nothing in this world is a coincidence! The same way that we can arrive at the number of four keys, and we already have discussed the significance of the number four."

"As in the four horsemen," Pearce reiterated.

"Which we might as well discuss in further detail because those four horsemen do relate directly to the four keys we just talked about."

"Is that so?" Pearce seemed surprised.

"The colors of those horses weren't by accident either. The first horse is white, under the guise of purity. White like the lamb John, but in this case, it represents a false holiness, armed with a golden bow, or a false covenant based on wealth, and it crowns itself in false pride and power. This is Lazarus's interpretation of the rival power that both threatened and challenged the Jerusalem Church for its governance over Christianity. He could foresee the death and suffering that would be wrought in its wake under the guise of purity and righteousness. That is exactly what the Damascus Church under Paul's authority did and that is your parallel to the first key. The second horse is red like the cloaks worn by the Roman military. Red like the rivers of blood shed by the world's mightiest military machine ever known. A military machine that dominated the world for seven hundred years. This horseman is only concerned with warfare and conquest. Living by the great sword, enemy to true peace and bringing about the destruction of the Jewish homeland as we saw with the second key. The third horse is black, based in darkness. This horseman does not attempt to prosper through the purity or holiness of the Judeo-Christian heritage. It is like a black wind that attempts to spread its darkness across the face of the earth. Black represents the symbolic and cultural significance of Islam. The black stone in the Kaaba in Mecca is venerated as a symbol of Allah's covenant. They touch it, they kiss it, the blackness considered sacred. The burdah or black cloak was worn by their prophet Mohammed, considered to be an outward display of modesty and piety. Beneath a black flag the Muslim armies fought their wars, the blackness of the flag said to be the idea of justice, unity and strength. Black is also associated in Islam with modesty, known as 'haya' and why their women are made to wear the niqab and abaya, to preserve their modesty. And in the horseman's hand it carries a balance. Not only symbolizing its pursuit to hold the balance of power, but also the ability to determine the fates of world economies because the world did not stop it from gaining control of vital resources. As a symbol of reverence and dignity, the colour reminds us of the constant battle between the forces of darkness and those of the light, and thus the third key is revealed. And lastly John, I need you to pay attention to the fourth horseman, mounted on its pale horse. It is without description. It is simply death. What it represents is beyond our imagination. We estimate, we speculate, but we cannot even fathom the destruction that this fourth beast can manifest. Nuclear holocaust, biological holocaust, world totalitarian government, how could we even attempt to comprehend death of this magnitude that is represented by that fourth key. Of course, it appears without color because the scourge of radiation or a bioweapon would be invisible to the naked eye. We cannot see the fourth horseman coming until it is too late. Four horsemen, four keys, four colors, the mark of the Beast is clearly evident."

CHAPTER FIFTEEN: THE GREAT ANNIHILATION

"We can ignore the first five sentences of chapter fourteen in Revelation because they are an obvious later insertion having nothing to do with the current status of the prophecy. The Tribulation, which was not part of the original book, had been discussed much earlier in our conversation, John, and timewise, it would take place before the battles ever occurred in order to protect the hundred and forty-four thousand."

"Yes, it does appear to be out of place, but that being the case, then why would they even bother to insert it here?"

"Because the story has taken on an entirely Jewish context after discussing the Beast. They would have realized that by now it appears that the sole purpose of the End of Days is the result of an effort to destroy the Children of Israel, and the Church editors were resistant to this non-Christian focus of the prophecy. How could they convince the world that Christianity was the one true religion of God was hanging on so tenaciously to the survival of his Chosen People. So, they did what anyone afraid of losing the story line would do; they threw in a reminder of what they wanted the story to be, even if it is pointing in a completely different direction and is embarrassingly out of place. What can I tell you, it was a panic move."

"I guess that sort of makes sense." Pearce analyzed my reasoning,

"As much as every other insertion they have made thus far. But you can't make a silk purse out of a sow's ear, as the old expression goes. It's just not kosher!" I couldn't resist telling that joke, no matter how bad it was. "Every attempt they're making to edit the story begins to look more and more ridiculous from this point forward. But the good news is that starting with sentence six, there is a shift in the story that they can't attempt to fix, and this is where I would suggest what I consider as being the starting point of chapter six of what was once the original text begins. Let me tell you what it says, '*And I saw another Angel flying in the midst of Heaven saying with a great voice, "Stand in awe of God and give him glory, because the hour of his judgment has come, and worship Him who made the Heavens and The Earth and the Sea and the springs of water.'*

"Except that my version doesn't read like that at all," Pearce pointed out. "You've left out the entire reference to preaching the gospel to the nations," he continued to explain, somewhat dismayed.

"Because it was never there," I addressed his concern. "The original Aramaic text made no such reference. Just a further example of how the Church editors were busy little beavers trying to damn the flood waters that were now washing away any hint of Christianity in the book. More importantly, this particular angel is announcing that God is no longer going to be a spectator to what has been taking place. The Almighty is finally going to defend the righteous. We see this in sentence eight where another angel makes the following announcement. *'And another, the second one, followed him and said, "Fallen, fallen, Babylon the Great, who gave all nations to drink of the passion of her fornication!'* You'll notice that the language of this sentence is somewhat different from your version as well. But what is important here is that the prophecy is finally pinpointing where the enemy's forces are gathering. As Babylon was the ancient capital of Mesopotamia, which we know today as Iraq, then we can now point clearly to the hotspots of this war. Follow the next few sentences closely because you will see how much they have been distorted from the original version, which I'm taking them from. *'Another, the third Angel, followed them saying with a great voice, "Whoever worshiped The Beast and its Image and received its mark on his forehead shall also drink from the wine of the passion of the Lord YAHWEH, which is mixed without dilution in the cup of his rage, and he will be tormented by fire and brimstone. And the smoke of their torment ascends for the eternity of eternities, and there is no rest, day or night, for those who worship the Beast and its Image and for him who takes the mark of its name. Here is the patience of the Holy Ones, those who keep the commands of God and the faith in YAHWEH."* You may think the changes in your King James version are subtle but if you examine them closely, there is a world of difference. Besides substituting Jesus's name for Yahweh, they completely obscure the fact that it's not the 'saints' as written in your book, but everyone that has remained faithful, as in all those that remained followers of God, adhering and enduring in their beliefs, no matter how bad things got. These are the Holy Ones being referred to; everyday people that remained loyal to the faith, not just a few saints as the editors wanted you to believe. But don't make the mistake of thinking these three angels are coming one immediately after the other, though it may appear that way from the structure of the sentences. The length of time between their appearances could be quite long, and the smoke of their torment doesn't happen until there's a decision to finally carpet bomb the enemy."

"Carpet bomb as in blowing everything up?" Pearce questioned.

"Carpet bombing is in everything and everyone," I confirmed. "Underlying these few sentences is a decision to finally accept that collateral damage of civilians could no longer be avoided and as a result the level of destruction rains down like fire and brimstone, touching everyone which is the meaning of His wrath is poured out without dilution. Pay particular attention to sentence thirteen because it is informing us that the losses on the side of those that are fighting for God will also be horrendous, but there is no mention of their having a reward in heaven, only that we must remember them. Going way back to where our discussion began, this would reinforce the original belief in Judaism, that there was no heaven, only the Shekinah."

Pearce was stunned into silence as he came to the realization that so much of his King James Bible was a distortion of the original manuscript. "I guess you're going to tell me that the Son of Man isn't riding on a cloud in the next sentence."

"I will, but first I have to remind you that the expression the Son of Man came from Ezekiel, and he used it in reference to himself. In the Book of Ezekiel, the term

'Son of Man' written as Ben Adam is used repeatedly by God to address the prophet, Ezekiel. If you were to count it, that phrase appears over ninety times in the book. God calling him that serves several purposes. The first is to remind Ezekiel of his human nature in contrast to God's divine nature. It also underscores his role as a representative of humanity, emphasizing that he is a mortal tasked with delivering God's message but possesses no power of his own. Secondly, by addressing Ezekiel as 'Son of Man,' God highlights Ezekiel's role as a prophet and intermediary between God and the people of Israel. The title serves as a constant reminder of Ezekiel's responsibility to faithfully communicate God's visions and judgments. And lastly, the title keeps Ezekiel grounded in his human limitations, even as he receives extraordinary divine revelations. It reminds him that his mission is not about personal glory but about serving God's purposes. Unfortunately, Christian theophiles decided to turn the title into something more than it was intended, attempting to say that anyone that used that title for Jesus was making reference to his demi-god status. Completely erroneous and it obscured the true meaning of this sentences which originally didn't even mention the 'Son of Man' but said the following: *'And behold, a white cloud, and upon the cloud sat the likeness of a man, and he had on his head a crown of gold, and in his hand a sharp sickle. And another Angel went out from the Temple and shouted with a great voice to him sitting on the cloud, "Send your sickle and reap, because the hour to reap has come." And he who sat on the cloud thrust his sickle unto The Earth and The Earth was reaped.'* It would appear that the man sitting on the cloud was based on Rabbinic beliefs from that time that the Messiah was a pre-existent being. This belief is recorded in the Talmud which suggests that the name or soul of the Messiah was created before the world itself. In Pesikta Rabbati 152b it lists the Messiah as one of the seven things created before the world. According to Sanhedrin 98b there is a discussion of the Messiah as a suffering figure who exists in every generation, waiting to be revealed. And in the Midrashic texts, there is a portrayal of the Messiah as someone already present in a hidden form or residing in the heavenly realm until the appointed time of redemption. Even though the Talmud didn't appear until almost two hundred years after the Book of Revelation was written, these apparitions of a Messiah already were common to the general beliefs of the populace. A human like figure sitting up in heaven, not yet fully formed into existence, had existed among the Pharisees and was derived from Isaiah 11:1-10, which they interpreted as meaning there was a future ideal ruler from the line of David. waiting in heaven, that was preordained and will emerge in a time of desperate needing peace and divine justice. So, from a religious context, that would be the rationale for someone with the likeness of a man floating around on a cloud with a sickle in his hand waiting to slaughter thousands upon thousands on the earth. I doubt that is precisely the image that you hope to see when you're thinking about your Jesus."

"You mean as a stone-cold killer," Pearce completed my thought concerning this man in the clouds. "You're right, that's not the Jesus I worship."

"But that is the nature of this figure resembling a man, sitting on a cloud. He is there for one reason only, and that is to kill as many of the enemy as he can. He represents vengeance, and that makes him more aligned to the Jewish context of the Messiah."

"Are you actually saying that you believe in the coming of a Messiah that isn't there to bring peace but instead represents death," Pearce challenged my own beliefs.

"Maybe there has to be a slaughter before you can have peace," I responded. "I believe it is the prophecy's way of saying that the death and destruction of the enemy will not happen directly via an intervention by God, but it will be done by God-fearing men. This figure is in the likeness of a man because he does represent the faithful of mankind that are willing to go to war. And what is 'the deliverer' anyway besides a man that dispatches our enemies. I can live with that concept."

"You know, you could have just said yes to my question." Pearce smiled.

"If I just said yes, then your next question would have been to ask me why. I just preempted you. If I happen to have a gut feeling, then I want to share that information. How else am I going to convince you that my interpretation has a high percentage of being correct."

"Then good luck with the remaining sentences of this chapter because even in Sunday school, my teachers couldn't provide a good explanation." Pearce continued his challenge with a faint laugh, thinking that even a gut feeling would not be enough to resolve some of the most difficult paragraphs found in Revelation.

"Probably because they were working from a mistranslation," I suggested. Here's what it says in the Aramaic, '*Another Angel went out from The Temple which is in Heaven, and there was with him a sharp sickle. Another Angel went out from the altar, who had authority over fire, and he shouted with a great voice to him who had the sharp sickle with him: "Send your sharp sickle and gather of the clusters of the vineyards of The Earth, because its grapes are large." And the Angel thrust his sickle unto The Earth and gathered the vines of The Earth and cast them into the great winepress of the passion of God. And the winepress was trodden outside the city and blood came out of the winepress unto the bridle of the horses for twelve thousand stadia.*'

"Yeah, that's exactly what I meant," Pearce groaned. "Makes no sense at all. According to most, it's just gibberish. What does making wine from large grapes have to do with any oof this?"

"I think it will make sense to you if we think of the angel with the sickle reaping souls and the one with the fire from the altar being the weapon of mass destruction. Now think back to the time of Lazarus. Every major city had a hippodrome, usually built close to the center of the city, and referred to as the Bridle because that is where the horses were haltered in the stables. What you may find interesting is that my ancient version uses stadia, but your more modern version uses furlongs. They were almost equivalent but someone when writing your version didn't know that and thought the 12,000 stadia was only equal to 1600 furlongs. But we know now that twelve thousand stadia would have been about 2250 kilometers. In furlongs it would have been about 2400 kilometers. What I see is this sentence suggesting that whatever this weapon was that they used, it falls down from the sky like fire from a heavenly altar and has a damage radius that extends outward for that distance of about 2400 kilometers. A weapon of that magnitude dropped on Baghdad would be felt as far off as Turkey, Egypt, Israel, Jordan, Saudi Arabia, Yemen, Oman, Iran, Afghanistan and the southern states of the Russian Federation. This truly is a doomsday weapon that the west unleashes on its enemies. This fact is evident in the first sentence of chapter fifteen which reads, *'And I saw another great and wonderful sign in Heaven: Angels which had the seven last plagues with them, for in them the anger of God is finished.'* It's a short chapter but we can imagine what those seven plagues were. As a result of the radiation poisoning there would be irreparable skin damage to those in the blast zone, famine from the crop devastation, the contamination of all drinking water, an almost incalculable death of farm animals, birth defects in the babies being born, cancer spreading at an incredible rate, and finally the last plague which would be death itself but that may have been a blessing and a mercy to those that died quickly and didn't suffer from the other plagues.

"A quick death would be preferable," Pearce admitted. "So, what's next?"

"Next is more poor editing by the Church's redactors. You will notice that the presence of a separate chapter sixteen as it appears I your version serves absolutely no purpose, as it was merely a confirmation of what was already written in the previous chapter. *'And the first went and poured his vessel upon The Earth, and there were severe and painful abscesses over the people who have the mark of The Beast upon them and over those who worship its image.'* Once again, it is describing the plague that manifests itself as radiation burns and sickness. Then it says, *'And the second Angel poured his vessel into The Sea and The Sea became as dead, and every living animal in the sea died,'* which confirms the second plague that resulted from contamination of the water. *'And the fourth Angel poured his vessel over the Sun, and it was given to him to scorch people with fire. And the children of men were scorched with great heat, and they blasphemed the name of God who has authority over these plagues, and they did not repent to give him glory,'* Simply describing the skin damage to those caught in the flash zone. But still, *'They blasphemed the name of The God of Heaven due to their pains and due to their sores, and they did not repent of their works.'* Even though they had been made to suffer horribly, they still would not surrender pursuing their evil ways. *'And the sixth Angel poured his vessel over the great river Euphrates, and its waters dried up that the way of the Kings from the East may be prepared.'* Here's proof that the suffering extends to all the nations considered to be part of the Middle East; if not as a direct result of the bomb, then from all the aftereffects created by the explosion.

"You're describing a huge area being affected," Pearce calculated the radius in his head. "Even those countries that weren't even involved, sounds like they are destroyed to some degree too along with the rest."

"It would seem that way," I agreed. "Just remember, I'm doing the interpreting, but Lazarus is the one doing the describing. Maybe it was a miscalculation, and they didn't know how powerful this bomb was. You just have to read sentence seventeen onward and you can see that the extent of the devastation is horrendous. *'And the seventh Angel poured his vessel into the air, and a great voice went out from The Temple* from before the throne, which said, "It is done." And there were lightnings and thunders and there was a great earthquake, the like of which earthquake there has not been since people have been upon The Earth, it was so great. And the great city became three parts, and the cities of the nations fell and Babylon The Great was remembered before God, to give it the cup of the wine of his passion and of his wrath. And every island fled, and the mountains were not found. And great hailstones, about a talent, fell from the sky on the children of men, and the children of men cursed God because of the plague of hail, because his plague was very great.' From the description it sounds like an admission that far more than just the enemy were caught up in the destruction, whether it be by accident or intent. The comment that the children of men cursed God, does not appear to be limited to only that population which wore the mark of the Beast. I do believe that the destructive power of the weapon unleashed had been underestimated and as a result, millions of unintended deaths occurred. Not that I'm squeamish about it but the question even I must ask myself, are we able to justify victory at any cost?"

"And what's your answer Doc?"

"Sadly, my answer has to be yes. The world squandered any past opportunities to avoid these events. Now, the revelations of Lazarus appear to be unavoidable, even though I keep telling myself this is only what can happen and not necessarily what will happen if we can find a way to change the future. But it's not as if we didn't see this coming. We chose to ignore all the hints. Thus far we've turned a blind eye to all the warning signs. We placed our faith in failed men rather than in the moral teachings of our ancestors. We looked to the pundits of political correctness and moral revisionists only to find that they have been serving their own agenda all along. Maybe we can still find a way to avoid the prophecy. Perhaps this change of direction in the political wind at the end of 2024 is our last chance to avoid catastrophe. I don't know the answer, John. All I know is we have to do something because we are facing a moral dilemma. If a prophecy is about what will happen if we don't change our ways, that would still mean it doesn't have to come to fruition if we can make some crucial changes."

"What kind of changes Doc?"

"That's the part where I'm stumped," I admitted. "I don't really know."

CHAPTER SIXTEEN: THE HARLOT

"You would think from the extent of the devastation resulting from that last bomb that it would signal the end of the war.   But apparently that's not the case when you read the beginning of chapter seventeen. '*And one of the seven Angels who had with them the seven vessels, came and spoke with me saying, "Follow me; I shall show you the judgment of The Harlot who sits on many waters,*' Even that sounds like it should be all over and Lazarus was being asked to come witness how the enemy had been destroyed.   Babylon as the harlot was about to be judged for her crimes. Everything about this sentence is in the past tense, so it's only logical to assume that the war must be over. A view supported by the next sentence where it says, '*For the Kings of The Earth committed fornication with her and all Earth dwellers are drunk with the wine of her fornication,*' indicating that those that she had gathered around her were no longer present because they are referred to in the past sense.   But that all suddenly changes when Lazarus is brought as an astral projection to wherever this location may be, as there is no mention of Babylon, and it would be reasonable to assume that the Harlot was dead, only to find out that she appears to be alive and well, while riding on a demonic beast."

"How is that even possible," Peace wondered.

"I'm asking the same thing. The only answer that I can arrive at is that the bomb only took out one of the prime areas of the Beast's army including its chief city, along with almost everything else in a two-thousand-kilometer radius but we need to remember there are other areas throughout the world that were part of this wicked alliance that weren't located in the Middle East. Places like Moscow, Beijing, Pyongyang, and possibly even Istanbul weren't affected. Like the hydra, you might cut off one head, but it just grows back two for everyone it loses. And that's what I believe is meant by her sitting on a multi-headed beast. Just as it says, '*And he brought me to the wilderness in the spirit, and I saw a woman who sat on a blood-red beast full of blasphemous names, which had seven heads and ten horns. And the woman was wearing purple and scarlet gilt with gold and precious stones and pearls and had a cup of gold in her hand, and it was full of abominations and the filth of her fornication.*' This harlot appears to be the supreme power in their alliance, a rich and powerful nation, that wear's the purple and scarlet colors of the aristocracy, adorned in precious jewels and gilt in gold. Even though I mentioned the capitals of those other nations, I have this strong feeling of betrayal as if this harlot was not the one from Babylon, nor even one of the original axis of evil partners but perhaps from a Western nation that turns its back on its alliance with the forces fighting on behalf of God."

"A traitor? What makes you think that?" Pearce was extremely curious about my intimation.

"Having her name written as 'Mystery Babylon' I think might be the biggest clue. We find that reference in sentence five. *'And upon her forehead was written: "Mystery Babylon, the Great, the Mother of Harlots and of the Filth of The Earth." And I saw the woman who was drunk with the blood of The Holy Ones and with the blood of the witnesses and I was stunned with a great astonishment when I saw her.'* Using the adjective mystery implies that we should think of her as being unknown or unexpected. What could be more unexpected than one of the nations we considered as an ally, fighting alongside us against the darkness, all of a sudden turning against us and supporting the Axis of Evil. That would be the ultimate mystery."

"Any suggestions as to which nation you think it might be?" Pearce prodded me to provide more information.

"I know this is going to sound wild, and you're probably going to consider me crazy, but I think it might be Britain that flips and betrays its partners in the Western alliance."

"That's insane," Pearce obviously did think my suggestion was crazy.

"Maybe, maybe not. There are certain clues that are provided," I attempted to defend my answer.

"Such as?" Pearce was not about to let me get away with my conjecture without an explanation.

"First, it says this Harlot sits on many waters. Babylon or Baghdad sits between two rivers, hardly what would be referred to as many waters. But that expression of sitting on many water is usually reserved to indicate seas and an island is thought to sit upon the sea. And anyone can tell you that the United Kingdom does sit on many seas. The Atlantic Ocean, the North Sea, the outlet of the Baltic Sea and the Arctic Ocean."

Pearce shook his head. "Still not enough Doc."

"Well, then there's the mention that the Kings of the Earth fornicated with her. Britannia as the symbol of the English kingdom is always going to be seen as the iconic image of an Empire that extended across the entire globe. Many rulers had sworn their allegiance to the British throne and at one time the Commonwealth was the largest empire to ever exist, and it was all due to its sea power."

Pearce was still shaking his head.

"Okay, think about this. The angel carries Lazarus's astral form into the wilderness, which is another way of saying unknown lands. Lazarus would have been familiar with everything around the Mediterranean, as well as the Middle East. That would not have been a wilderness to him, but the British Isles certainly would have been unfamiliar."

The expression on Pearce's face had changed and appeared more thoughtful. "Better," was all that he said.

"Finally, it's the use of the term the Great Mother, to paraphrase the last sentence. That was a term that was used when the colonies referred to Queen Victoria. I'm not saying definitively that Lazarus is pointing us towards Britain, but there certainly are enough clues that might suggest it."

This time Pearce nodded his head. "You might be on to something Doc."

"Here's something else to keep in mind. In 2021 the Muslim population in England was just under 2 million. Three years later it has doubled to 4 million. That's almost 7 percent of the total population. That number is predicted to be just under 20 percent to 50 percent by the year 2050. We talked about this final war being a generational war that does not end quickly. Could we still be fighting it by the year 2050? Based on the war in Afghanistan, the answer to that question could easily be yes. Would a population that could be anywhere from one out of five British citizens to one out of two swing the country's allegiance to the other side if the war continues for that long? I think it would be highly possible!"

"But that is just one possible scenario. Doesn't mean it will necessarily be that way," Pearce postulated. "But I'm not saying that it couldn't be."

"And that is exactly what the angel says to Lazarus starting with sentence seven. *'And the Angel said to me, "Why are you stunned? I shall tell you the mystery of The Woman and of The Beast that bears her, which has seven heads and ten horns. The Beast which you saw, existed and is not, and is about to come up from the Sea, and is going to destruction. And the inhabitants on Earth will marvel, whose names are not written in The Book of Life from the foundation of the world, when they see The Beast which was, and is not, and is approaching.'* He's saying the beast may exist but does not exist yet. He's saying the potential exists but is not yet realized, but it will happen if not stopped now from happening. On that, I believe the angel is pretty crystal clear."

"Okay. I sort of can grasp that maybe is and maybe not scenario from what was said, but if that's the case, then how do you make sense of the sentences afterwards. When you put them together, they don't seem to point to your conclusion."

"You mean the detail in the ninth sentence, such as, *'Here is the meaning for one having wisdom: the seven heads are seven mountains, upon which The Woman sits. And there are seven Kings; five have fallen and one remains, and there is another not yet come, and when he comes, a little remaining time is given to him.'* Is that what you're referring to?"

"Especially that part," Pearce confirmed.

"The angel is telling you right from the start that the person that deciphers this clue is the exception and not part of the mainstream pundits that think they know what it says."

"By pundits you're referring to the Christian churches. Bit of a put down, don't you think?"

"You said that. I didn't say that. If I said to you the seven mountains were seven hills, what would be your immediate thought?"

"The seven hills of Rome."

"And when we think of Rome, we immediately think of one of the greatest empires that ever existed. Therefore, the seven heads each represent an empire, with Rome as the starting point from which they were spawned. Five of these have passed into history and one currently is in power. Rome, Byzantium, Holy Roman Empire representing all the various European empires, the Mongol-Russian empire representing all the Eastern empires, and the Ottoman Empire representing all of the Islamic empires. Currently, we can think of American world domination as the empire that is currently holding the reigns of the world, but it is weakening rapidly."

"That's six," Pearce announced.

"Right. That means one more to come. But when the seventh comes, there is very little time allotted to its domination, and the reason for that is because we enter shortly afterwards into Armageddon. But to know who this seventh one is, you need to refer to my Aramaic version because the clue is missing from your version of Revelation. Sentence eleven says, *'And the Dragon, and the Beast which it brought and is not, also is the eighth, and is of the seven, and is going to destruction.'* Take the dragon literally as this tells you precisely who the seventh short-lived empire will be; it's China. Your text is missing this reference to the dragon. And we just discussed the possible threat that is not yet present but may exist in the future, but this should not be viewed as a separate attempt at world dominance but is only an extension of this seventh empire. As it says, this rise to dominance will only result in destruction, which indicates that the final war will break out soon. Once you understand that the Beast that is not, is merely an extension of this short-lived Chinese empire, then you will immediately understand the next sentence."

"Slow down a bit Doc, you're losing me here. You're saying the seventh is China but somehow it counts as the eighth because it's a beast?"

"No, no, no," I shook my head. "It's still the seventh, but because soon after its rise to power the world rolls into the final war, the so-called beast, it transitions into the next phase. By calling it the eighth, it's only emphasizing how short the reign of the seventh empire is."

"I think I got it," but Pearce didn't sound too certain.'

"So, as I was saying, what comes next is: *'And the ten horns of the Beast are ten Kings, whose Kingdoms they have not yet received, but take authority as Kings for one hour with the Beast.'* As the beast is now synonymous with the Chinese attempt at world domination, it has only one hour, implying a very short lifespan, in which to inflict havoc on the world. China is not alone, as we have long discussed concerning the Axis of Evil, but all together it is supported by ten other nations that all dedicate their support and forces to China as seen in sentence thirteen. After that the war breaks out, which ultimately the forces of evil lose. And then the angel does something strange beginning with sentence fifteen, in that it appear that he senses that Lazarus has not been following the story line successfully, sort of like yourself, and the angel feels the need to give him even more clues. *'And he said to me, "The waters that you saw, upon which The Harlot sat, are the nations, multitudes, peoples and languages. And the ten horns that you saw on The Beast will hate The Harlot and will make her desolate and naked and will devour her flesh and will burn her in fire. For God gave into their hearts to perform his pleasure and to do their one purpose and will give their Kingdom to that Beast until the words of God are fulfilled. And The Woman which you saw is that Great*

City, which has rule over the Kings of The Earth.' At first all it does is make it sound even more confusing. If the Harlot was riding the Beast, and the dragon unleashed the Beast, then why would the ten nations that were supposedly supporting the dragon suddenly turn on the Harlot. Doesn't seem to make sense, does it?

"No, it doesn't," Pearce agreed. "Doesn't make sense at all."

"Except it does," I challenged his comment. "Remember who I told you I suspected this Harlot was," I instructed.

"You said you thought it was Britain."

"And all of this just supports my supposition that the mysterious harlot is England. The angel explains the many waters does refer to the Harlot's empire including many nations that spoke completely different languages. Despite their differences, the Harlot was able to hold them together, but then it made its biggest mistake. Britain invited everyone from the Commonwealth nations to come live in United Kingdom. Suddenly, Britain wasn't English any longer. But the beast, to which it is contributing its forces too, as I discussed earlier, is comprised of countries that when combined have two hundred million Muslims, none of whom have any love for England and that hatred has slowly been seeping into the population inhabiting the British Isles. They have no desire to preserve its institutions, which the angel describes as stripping her bare, devouring her flesh and incinerating her with fire. All that Britain once was, will be destroyed and replaced. Her constitution will be shredded, her justice system violated, and her religious institutions demolished."

"Wow!" Pearce gasped. "You seem pretty confident in expecting the demise of England, far more than just a suspicion."

"I can only tell you what I see, and these are the images that dance through my head when I read this section. But I emphasize once again, this is not necessarily what will be. It can be stopped if we consciously make the decision to do so."

"Doc, the only way you could stop it is by turning back the clock and erasing all the mistakes that have taken place thus far. And since you can't turn back time, I think you're whistling a pipe dream."

"Maybe I am, John, maybe I am."

CHAPTER SEVENTEEN: THE ENEMY WITHIN

'And after these things I saw another Angel from Heaven, who had great authority, and The Earth was brightened by his glory. And he shouted with a great voice: "Fallen, fallen, Babylon the Great! And it is become the abode for Demons and a prison to every impure and detestable spirit. Because she mixed of the wine of her fornication for all the nations, and the Kings of The Earth committed fornication with her, and the merchants of The Earth have become rich by the power of her mad infatuation.' Not much different here at the beginning of Chapter 18 that you haven't already heard before, John.

"Then why did he bother to write it again?"

"To emphasize that there were a lot of people supporting that side of the equation. That's the peculiarity regarding world politics. We'd like to think that we're on the right side, the pillars of freedom and the staunch supporters of liberty. We love God and we claim the moral high ground. But you'd be surprised to know that those on the other side think exactly the same way about their existence. In their eyes, we're the corrupt and evil ones. We'd like to think that they're all enslaved by their governments, having no choice in the matter but having lived in China for as long as I have, I can tell you that is not the case. As the angel says, there is an entire stratum of their society that is accumulating power and riches. One of the hardest things for us to consider is that our enemies may actually be benefitting and enjoying their lives under the governance of what we consider an evil empire far more than some of the people living within our institutions. It's only our opinion that says they're bad and evil but that is not necessarily the viewpoint from the other side."

"But we're the side that believes in freedom and democracy. They lack those qualities in their lives. Once they have experienced them, they will then know that they live under brutal regimes."

"That's our perspective, not necessarily theirs. For example, we both believe in God but not exactly in the same way and I don't think no matter how long we discuss our beliefs, either of us will agree fully with the other."

"That's different," John insisted. "We may not believe in the same manner as how we've been delivered the message or how we practice our religions but when it comes to adhering to our moral values and the basics required to follow a path of enlightenment, and doing good deeds, then we are no different."

"And if they should share a morality and belief system that is alien to us, but strongly held by them, why should they at any point consider themselves as being wrong. And that is what is defined in the next few sentences. *'And I heard another* voice from Heaven that said, "Come out from within her my people, lest you share in her sins, that you would not receive from her plagues. Because the sins in her have touched Heaven, and God has called her evil to mind Pay her just as she also has paid and give her double for her deeds. In the cup which she has mixed, mix her a double. Because of that in which she glorified and exalted herself, give such suffering and sorrow, for she said in her heart, 'I sit a queen, and I am not a widow, and I shall not see sorrow.'" Because of this, in one day there will come upon her plagues, death, sorrow, and starvation, and she will burn in fire, because the Lord Yahweh is powerful who judges her.' It is only according to our Judeo-Christian beliefs that we condemn this other empire as being wrong and their beliefs as sinful. But it is the fact that they will not tolerate any other belief by which we condemn them, and so we tell all of those that believe like us to leave her domain lest they suffer the consequences of our war against that empire. Yet, from the angel's statement, it is clear that there are many that may have the same belief system as us, but because they are receiving benefits from their association, they are reluctant to leave her domains. Paying her double is the angel's way of saying take the loss, give up whatever benefits you believe you are receiving and return to the land from whence you came. That's a hard pill to accept. There are many like me that are doing very well financially by living in the belly of the beast."

"But you would certainly leave if the final battle at the End of Days came about," Pearce was questioning how I would deal with the situation.

"I probably wouldn't have a choice but when that time comes, I know I would want to be on that next plane back to New Zealand, leaving behind all the friends and acquaintances I have made over the years in China. Friends that would never understand why I was leaving."

"Wouldn't it be obvious to them?"

"Not at all. As it said in the paragraph I just read to you, the Queen protests that she does not see herself doing any wrong but in the end, it is we who judge her according to our beliefs and our fundamental faith in God."

"It sounds like you think that we might be the bad guys as well," Pearce reflected on what I had just said.

"We have our beliefs and our principles. They have theirs. We fundamentally disagree, and it appears that both sides according to the prophecy will be unable to find a compromise. It is clear that they are the intolerant ones, and unwilling to accept our presence with our way of life. That is clear from all the opening chapters in Revelation. That being the case, then I guess you can call them the bad guys. But now we are looking at the second phase of this war. There's already been massive destruction as we've discussed earlier. There may have been an opportunity to rebuild and cool own the rhetoric but beginning with sentence eleven it is clear that we are now intent on total obliteration of these enemy states. 'And the merchants of The Earth will weep and grieve over her, and there is no one buying their cargo again: Cargo of gold and silver and of precious stones, of pearls, of fine linen, of purple, of silk, of scarlet, of every fragrant wood and every ivory vessel, every precious wooden vessel, and brass, iron *and marble. Cinnamon, spices, ointments, frankincense, wine, oil, fine white flour, sheep, horses, chariots and the bodies and souls of the children of men. And your own pleasant fruits have departed from you, and everything luxurious and splendid is gone from you and you will not see them again. And the merchants of these things, who grew rich by her, will not find them, and they will stand opposite from fear of her punishment, weeping and lamenting, and saying, "Alas alas, the great city that wore fine linen and purple and scarlet gilt in gold and precious stones and pearls! For the wealth is lost in one hour!" In this way also, every ship Navigator, everyone traveling in a ship to places, and the ship Captains, and everyone who does business at sea, stood from a distance, And they lamented her when they saw the smoke of her burning and they were saying, "Who is like The Great City?" And they cast earth upon their heads and shouted as they wept and lamented and they were saying, "Alas, alas, Great City, by which those who had ships in the sea grew rich from her magnificence, which is destroyed in one hour!"* Just goes to prove that wars are settled by which side runs out of money to support their war effort first."

"You're suggesting that Armageddon comes to a conclusion because their bank account runs dry first. How's that a victory of good over evil?: Pearce was perplexed by the outcome.

"It's not," I concurred. "It's just reality and it happens to be what the angel, as you can clearly see, tells Lazarus. Initially, we want to believe that if this war takes place then it will be a war that we become engaged in based upon a simple principle of good versus evil, but like so many other wars in our time, it appears to have shifted gears into this second phase, entirely based on economic competition. I'm with you, I find this chapter disturbing. I would even go as far as saying hypocritical. We were led to believe that it was about eliminating the forces of evil and by this chapter it's nothing but the destruction of the markets, trade and commerce of what we had labeled an evil empire. The chapter focuses entirely on the consequences of their economic downfall, particularly from the perspective of those who once profited from its wealth and trade and now abandon it. This emphasis on commerce and the lamentation of merchants and the powerful elite certainly highlights a narrative centered and more concerned about economic principles rather than the moral and spiritual failings of our world."

"Perhaps it is intended as a juxtaposition of Babylon's material wealth versus the spiritual riches of God's kingdom with the focus on trade and commerce serving to remind us of the transient nature of earthly wealth and possessions as compared to the eternal values promoted by the divine," Pearce raised a good argument even if it did sound like a desperate one.

"I don't deny that wealth, commerce and political alliances are the worldly mechanisms that sustain evil systems, but what I didn't want to be told was that this war was extended as a result of trade, competition, greed and exploitation. To accept that we will continue to kill like rabid animals for reasons other than protecting the people, their rights and dignity, as well preserving our own lives which are being threatened, I can't defend in principle. Should it be true that a significant proportion of the reasons for engaging in this conflict was that those in our governments had weighed our own deaths and losses against an economic bottom line, then I will be furious as a result of the deception. It would shatter my faith in mankind. What may have begun as a battle between good and evil, would no longer serve that purpose. If what the angel has just said is true, then we have even more reason to find a way to ward off this prophecy from taking place. If we don't, we may lose our souls as well when it is all over."

"It's almost as if we will become the enemy. Pursuing a path that we condemned those on the other side of perpetuating. We'd be as bad as them. Even worse!"

"I only can look at sentence twenty and wonder why it was written in the manner in which it was. *Rejoice over her, Oh Heaven, Holy Ones, and Prophets, because God has executed your judgement upon her!*' Why isn't it God's judgement. Isn't that how this all began? Because God passed judgement on the beast that rose up against all of his followers and threatened the Children of Israel. When did it suddenly become the judgment of men as symbolized by the Holy Ones and Prophets."

"It doesn't say that in my King James version," Pearce attempted to correct me. "It says that God has avenged them on her."

"Of course it does," I told him. "Whomever was performing the editing saw the same thing I did when reading the Aramaic version. They immediately would have said it had to be a mistake, so they changed it."

"You think they wouldn't dare to have been that brazen."

"Why not? That's my point. Men make mistakes and errors in judgement all the time. We are fallible. We are inherently going to war for all the wrong reasons. A church editor will change a sacred text simply because he doesn't like the way it reads. That so-called Holy Man knew exactly what he was doing, the same way I believe Lazarus knew exactly what the angel was saying. But in all of this, when did God abrogate his involvement as judge and hand it over to the men involved?"

"We have to trust that we entered into this war for all the right reasons," he insisted. "Maybe we lose sight of those initial reasons the longer the war continues. But we have to believe the Lord wouldn't let us continue to fight under false pretenses."

"But can we believe that?" I had my doubts. "The motives may change over time. as indicated in the sentence which says that the continuation of the war was to be based not on instructions from God but instead, we are told to continue to fight because of a judgement made by men. The rest of the chapter only serves to confirm that the decision is solely human in its embodiment and not divinely inspired. . Here's what it says exactly: *'And one of the Angels took a mighty stone, great as a millstone, and cast it into the sea and said, "In this way with violence, Babylon the Great City will be thrown down, and it will not exist again! And the sound of stringed instruments and of trumpets and the various singers and shouting will not be heard in you again. And the light of a lamp will not appear to you again, and the voice of a groom and the voice of a bride will not be heard in you again, because your merchants had been great ones of The Earth, for by your sorceries you deceived all the nations!" And in her was found the blood of The Prophets and Holy Men who were murdered on Earth.'* Note that the emphasis once again is on the wealth of this enemy empire with its music, and festive lights, and lavish weddings but at least it ends by saying that all this was a false front as a cover for all of its lies, murders, and deceit upon which they built their empire. That's the only redeeming statement that indicates it wasn't predicated entirely on economics but was the result of their evil ways, which in turn just happened to make them wealthy and patrons of the arts."

"Are you saying that sometimes we just have to believe that whatever we do, we do it for all the right reasons, Doc, even if it doesn't always seem that way?"

"When you say it that way, it sounds pretty pathetic." I admitted. "Almost as if we can be so easily brainwashed into believing what others say and not checking it out for ourselves. But isn't that a fitting description of who we are today. An entire generation that would rather believe what they hear on social media rather than investigate and research the facts themselves. All I can tell you is that we can never let go of our own moral compass. Not at any cost. That to me is a certainty. I have no doubt about that John, and I can assure you my faith in God is strong. But our putting faith in mankind, that is perhaps where we might find reasons to be a little dubious. I know instinctively that Lazarus saw what he wrote in his book, but I also know that so much of the text was changed that it is not always that easy to separate what was delivered to him by God and what was written by men."

"You're the one that has been insisting all this time that your Aramaic version is far more accurate. Wouldn't that mean that if it's in your book than it must have been their originally?"

"More accurate, yes, but do I know if it was the original manuscript, the first version ever written, that I can't tell you. All I can say is that the Greek versions that the King James bible used came much later and therefore are less accurate and have been edited and altered far more extensively."

"That being the case, then maybe all this talk about continuing the war for the sake of economic dominance was never in the original manuscript," Pearce suggested, as if that was true then it would make all of this controversy disappear.

"No, I'm pretty certain it was there," I disagreed. "Over time, any changes made to the book would have been for the purpose of increasing its religious fervor and pursuing a more fantastic style of imagery that would draw the reader into a greater perspective of Hell and in so doing, increase their fear of demonic domination."

"And you're saying because these sentences are not serving that purpose, not being sensationalist at all but rather being a somewhat boring dissertation on economic interactions means that it was probably always there."

"Precisely," I answered. "Providing a blurb on international marketing, as the angel has done, along with economic strategic warfare, hardly serves the purpose of increasing the imagery of the struggle against dark forces . Therefore, I do believe Lazarus did see or hear this part of the prophecy, because that is exactly what we do in our wars now, ever since the Viet Nam War. We are fighting battles now as if they were international trade wars, harming each other's natural resources, and hoping the government on the other side will collapse before our own does. That is the new rules of engagement in combat.

"But it's not right," Pearce responded. "War should only be about protecting the liberties and freedoms of the people."

"Was it ever about that?" I wondered.

"Maybe not," Pearce admitted, "But we're talking about Doomsday now, the final battle and therefore I has to be about conquering the forces of evil."

"Ah, yes, the ultimate battle of right and wrong, and here we are talking about economic warfare. Not saying it's the wrong, but it certainly isn't right!"

CHAPTER EIGHTEEN: THE AFTERMATH

"Time to bring this all to a close," I said, practically yawning at the same time. "This is where I think chapter seven would have begun in the original manuscript, and it would have been short and sweet."

"How can this be the final chapter. There's still four chapters left in my copy of Revelation."

"Isn't that amazing," I laughed. "I told you there were significant differences between the Aramaic version and what you're reading as Revelation."

"How's that even possible? These next few chapters are the most crucial ones," Pearce protested my dismissal of almost one fifth of the Book of Revelation. "They include the marriage of Jesus, followed by the entire army of angels riding on white horses to fight the forces of the Beast. Then they chain Satan for a thousand years in the pit, followed by the resurrection. Those events are critical to the prophecy! They're some of the best parts of the prophecy!'"

"Are they? I thought you would have realized the battle was over and done with when we discussed the last chapter. Every beast, harlot and king on the other side had already been destroyed or at least was about to be after the angel tossed down the millstone. That signified the war was over at that point. So, everything you just talked about couldn't happen, because for all intent and purpose, the had ended and there was no one left to fight. Or do you think there was actually two separate wars and this one is somehow unrelated to the first?."

"Same one," he insisted but this is simply description of the destruction that was left behind, followed by the punishment that the enemy received,"

"No, it's not!" I refuted his claim. "Your story talks about chaining the Devil, or Satan for a thousand years and then letting him loose so he can go out and deceive all the nations into what is then referred to as the final battle against Gog and Magog. Don't you think it's kind of strange that Jochanan or Eleazar, whichever name you want to choose, considered the last battle to be the one he had finished describing over the first eighteen chapters without any mention of the 'great' battle to occur later. Even according to your version, the original fight was the battle of Armageddon but now we're faced suddenly with round two, a thousand years later and this time it's with an enemy known as Gog and Magog. That makes absolutely no sense at all."

"Weren't you the one that said a thousand years to us could be like a day to God. If that's the case, this would be like tomorrow in God's mind." Pearce attempted to use my own words against me."

"If that's the case, then what was the final battle that we already experienced for eighteen chapters?"

"Perhaps it was a prelude, I guess," Pearce offered his own unfounded theory.

"Well guess again," I suggested. "What would say about that fact that we never have Satan named or even mention a being known as the Devil for those eighteen chapters and suddenly those words of Devil and Satan are appearing all over the place in chapter twenty of your book. Don't you find that odd?"

"Maybe two different versions of the same story," Pearce proffered his answer sheepishly..

"How about two different stories all together that someone decided to superimpose on each other because they wanted a more Christian setting and ending? Let's face it John, the Church chroniclers wanted this book desperately to be part of our canon and they would have gone to any lengths to make it so. Even fabricate an entirely new ending to the battle of Armageddon if that's what it took."

"I don't believe they would take it that far," Pearce was reluctant to face the truth.

"No, you don't think so. Well let's talk about Gog and Magag then.

"What about them?"

"They were taken from the book of Ezekiel, chapters thirty-eight and thirty-nine. No one knew who Ezekiel was referring to then, so adding them to Revelation served no other purpose than to extend the war against an unknown foe so that Jesus and Satan could be introduced to the book.

"But how do we know there couldn't be some other armies just waiting to attack once both sides fighting in the earlier war were exhausted and practically eliminated. It would be the perfect opportunity for them."

"For whom John? There's no one left. We've already seen every major force in the war engaged in the war that took place over the first eighteen chapters. The only thing left to launch an attack would be aliens from space."

"How can we be certain Magog doesn't represent a place that might still remain as a threat." I'll give Pearce this, he is persistent.

"Alright, let's say there is a Gog and he comes from a place Magog, where might it be. Ezekiel hinted they came from the North-East. That would suggest or even China, but they've already been defeated by this time. In the Quran, Gog and Magog are referred to as Yajuj and Majuj in Surah Al-Kahf and Surah Al-Anbiya. They were identified as a warrior people that were confined behind a great wall that was constructed b Dhul-Qarnayn around 300 BC. Now why does that sound familiar."

Pearce didn't respond.

"I wasn't being rhetorical then," I pointed out. "I was looking for an answer but I'll give it to you anyway. Third century BC the Emperor Qin Shi Huang orders the first major construction of the Great Wall of China. Once again we have a reference that Gog and Magog were the Chinese. And once again I remind you that they were defeated in the battle that was already described."

"That could be possible," Pearce admitted reluctantly. "But what then about the next chapter describing New Jerusalem descending from heaven?"

"Did someone forget that we already talked about rebuilding the Temple of New Jerusalem a long time ago, in the early chapters of the book? Maybe we're dealing with a small case of prophetic amnesia," I joked but I could see that Pearce was not laughing.

"You don't have to be sarcastic," Pearce sounded a little bit upset and disgruntled.

"Well, someone had to say these things because when something appears so fraudulent, it only serves to disparage the true value and essence of the original manuscript. Here's the problem John, you're reading a version that was translated from a much later copy known as the Textus Receptus, a Greek manuscript that was already known to include certain verses and phrasing that did not appear in earlier manuscripts or versions. That's just a fact and you can check it out with any theological expert. I'm working as you are aware from a different text known as the Aramaic Peshitta: The Peshitta is a Syriac translation of a much earlier manuscript, perhaps the original, and it is considered to be an ancient tradition that developed independently of the Greek texts."

"What is independent supposed to mean?"

"In other words, it wasn't influenced by the Church redactors and editors that worked for the Pope. In the technical language of religious historians that have commented, it is often described as being an earlier textual form that might omit expansions or clarifications added in later Greek copies. That is a round-about way of how the Church tries to account for the differences. Your copy they freely admit may contain expansions and clarifications that were added into the Greek copies. Simple English, there's a lot of false writing in the version you are reading and they know it."

"That's a little harsh, don't you think, calling it false. I'll need to check that out."

"I encourage you to do that. Don't just accept my word. I need you to research it so that you understand why I made the claim that this was never intended to be a Christian document originally."

"Like I said Doc, I'll check it out."

"You'll also find out that the Aramaic Peshitta is written in a more concise, straightforward style. In contrast, we know the King James translators often expanded phrases or added words for clarity or doctrinal emphasis based on their Greek source. They admitted that when they completed their task for the Anglican Church. This also will obviously account for variations in word choice. There are words in Hebrew and Aramaic that just don't have an English equivalent."

"That can account for word differences Doc, but you're talking about entire chapters not originally present that have been added. You're asking me to accept as fact that someone intentionally falsified something like twenty percent of the book."

"Because the Peshitta was transcribed from a much simpler, earlier tradition, it was only natural that over time, there were going to be things added and you have to remember that the Greek New Testament had a complex history of transmission, with numerous copies being made. Each time they made a copy, there were going to be minor variations. The Aramaic version followed a different path, leading to the absence or alteration of certain verses as compared to the later Greek manuscripts. That in itself is a Jewish rabbinic tradition that the copy must be identical to the original, or else it is to be destroyed. The Greek copies suffered from what is often termed as scribal decisions, which were either intentional or unintentional."

"What would an unintentional error be?"

"That's when they're copying a word, mistake a letter and suddenly it has an entirely different meaning," I answered, "but they still keep the copy in circulation."

"And intentional?"

"The Peshitta is missing a lot of the content that is in your version, especially Chapter 22. And one of the most interesting lines in the King James version is 22:19: which includes a stern warning about altering the text, which is almost hysterically funny when one thinks that is exactly what the editor did, by adding this section. What's even more hysterical, and I mean this in the way of being funny again, is how Christian Theologians will say that it's all because the Aramaic text is a more primitive version. Somehow the accuracy of being an early edition and only including what was originally said makes it primitive as if it is open to enhancement and therefore must be considered as incomplete until more modern editions with all their additions become available. In that way these modified editions would be considered as being more accurate and superior. That entire thought stream is so backwards that it's ludicrous. All that your later versions indicate is the influence of centuries of Greek textual evolution, providing what you might consider as being unique Christian perspectives on apocalyptic prophecy, but it certainly isn't accurate, and it most definitely isn't original or superior as they would suggest!"

"That being the case then, Doc, how does your version conclude Revelation?

"Very simply," I stated. "Lazarus has just described his vision of the downfall of the Harlot and the defeat of her empire in the wilderness and then he writes, '*And after these things, I heard a great sound of many multitudes in Heaven saying, "Hallelujah! Redemption, glory and power to our God! For His judgments are true and just, because He has judged The Great Whore, who corrupted The Earth with her whoredom, and He has required the blood of his Servants from her hand." Again, they said, "Hallelujah!" And her smoke ascends to the eternity of eternities. And the twenty-four Elders and The Four Beasts fell down and worshiped our God who sits on the throne, and they were saying, "Amen! Hallelujah!" And there was a voice from the throne that said, "Praise our God, all His Servants and worshipers of His name -- all of them, the small with the great!"* The most striking thing about it, which I know you must have definitely noticed is that there is absolutely no reference to Jesus. He doesn't play any role in the war or the aftermath. End of story."

"You're right, it is very simple," Pearce commented, "But it feels like it is missing so much."

"According to you. Why should it have been made overly complicated? The Beast is defeated. The Harlot has been executed. The evil empire has been obliterated and now all the heavens, along with the rest of us that have remained faithful are singing 'Hallelujah' and "Praise be to God!' It's a happy ending to what was looking at first to be a disastrous prophecy."

"Any more to it, or is that it?"

"A few more sentences," I instructed. "Next is: '*And I heard a sound like that of many multitudes, and like the sound of many waters and like the sound of mighty thunders saying, "Hallelujah! For the Lord Yahweh, God Almighty reigns!"*' The waters are quite symbolic because the first time we're introduced to the sea, we have an evil beast rising out of it. Now the seas are calm, and the praise sung on the voices of the people sound exactly like the waves on the water. Everything has returned to its natural state. This picturesque setting is followed by, '*And he said to me, "These words are trustworthy and true, and the Lord Yahweh, God of The Spirit of The Holy Prophets, has sent His Angel to show His Servants what is granted to happen soon.*' It is odd that this would be the first time that we're given an indication of the time period, and it is probably one of the reasons that Rabbi Akiva and others probably thought their battle against Rome, which is now known as the Bar Kochba War, was the right time. But who really knows what 'soon' means according to God's calendar."

"Well, I think anyone reading the word 'soon', would think it means in a short time to follow."

"Which is probably why the wording in your version changed it to say, '*The things that must shortly be done.*' That makes it much more vague, begging the question, exactly what things, as well as what does shortly mean. Things could refer to just spreading the word or making preparation and all that could take a very long time. It appears that the editors were worried that the people would pick up on the word 'soon' and be misled, thinking that when it didn't happen in their lifetime, it would cast doubt on the veracity of the scripture. This was their way of avoiding any controversy. Just remove the word 'soon'."

"Soon does mean soon," Pearce made this surprisingly intelligent comment. "Wouldn't that make the entire prophecy false because it didn't happen close to the time Jochanan wrote the book."

"I take it as a warning to every generation that reads the book that they should worry that it might be just around the corner for them. Lazarus had no way of knowing when the events he was seeing would take place. If the angel had said 'later' then no one would give it any consideration because they'd always believe it will happen much later and they had nothing to worry about, which is human nature. A prophecy that is not perceived as a present threat doesn't have much effect on the behavior of the people."

"A bit of a psychological ploy then."

"Perhaps. If God wants to instill good behavior, then all the people!, all the time need to understand the threat of a lack of morality and evil in society might bring about. But the one thing you don't want to induce is a lack of hope. Lazarus understood this when in the following sentences he said, '*I am Jochanan, who saw and heard these things. And when I saw and heard, I fell to worship before the feet of the Angel who was showing me these things. And he said to me: "Seer, no! I am your fellow Servant and of your brothers the Prophets and of those who observe these words of this book. Worship God!"*' Personally, I thought this would have been a beautiful place to end the book, but Lazarus still had a few more things he wanted to say about it."

"What's so great about that sentence," Pearce inquired.

"Everything. Firstly, it tells you that this entire story has been a direct communication between God and Jochanan or Lazarus. No one else involved and as I had mentioned right from the start, no Jesus. That is poignant, especially considering I've been making the argument that the book is intended as Jewish Apocrypha. Secondly, it reminds us that angels are no different from us. They are no different from the prophets or any faithful follower of Yahweh. Therefore, the practice of worshipping or praying to specific angels should be frowned upon, as it is an affront to God."

"You're saying then that the belief in guardian angels in wrong."

"I'm saying that people that pray to what they believe is their guardian angel is wrong. Angels do not merit prayer. That is exactly what Lazarus is being told in that sentence."

"Got it!"

"But as I stated, Lazarus seems to have this compulsion to keep on talking even though the prophecy is ended and in the next few sentences he writes, 'And He said to me, *Do not seal the words of the prophecy of this book, for the time is near and he who does evil, will do evil again; he who is foul, again will be polluted; the righteous again will do righteousness and the holy will again be hallowed. Behold, I come at once, and my reward is with me, and I shall give to every person according to his work. I am Aleph and I am Tau, The First and The Last, The Origin and The Fulfillment.*' One can see that he wanted to end the prophecy in the same manner that he began it, stating that God is omnipresent, and He is relying on Lazarus to ensure the prophecy becomes published. But the real interesting part is that according to God's message, he doesn't believe that publishing the book is going to change anyone or anything. An evil person will continue to do evil, and a good person will continue to be good. That to me sounds like there is no expectation of changing anyone's bad behavior. One might question what is the purpose of the prophecy then if nothing and no one is going to change."

"If that's true, then why do you believe the events of the prophecy can be prevented if God and his angels don't even believe it."

"A good question. Maybe I'm just an optimist, but I believe if we truly our good by nature, then at least we must make an effort to try and change the future for the better. Isn't that our purpose for being born into this world in the first place."

"I don't know Doc; do we have a purpose?"

"I hope so, because I'd hate to think that we're just wasting our time being on this earth for seventy or eighty years. If we are gifted with freewill then technically we should be able to make a difference."

"And if the future is pre-determined and fate can't be changed? Pearce always has to point out the downside.

"Then we have to pray the last few sentences in the book according to the Aramaic version is correct. '*Blessings to those who are doing his Commandments; their authority shall be over The Tree of Life, and they shall enter The City by the gates and outside are fornicators, murderers, idol worshipers, the defiled, sorcerers and all seers and workers of lies.*' Until the End of Days actually does occur, we're going to need to protect ourselves in God's sanctuary city because we can't dare to set one foot outside. And whether that city is referring to a country or countries, our security entirely relies on having a government in place that is motivated to do the right thing by its people."

"That will be a first," Pearce said sarcastically.

"Let's just hope it's not the last."

CHAPTER NINETEEN: IN CONCLUSION

"Do you mind if I ask you straight out Doc, what was this all about?

"Exactly what do you mean?"

"I flew over here because you told me to come, but as soon as I get here, you tell me you never called. And then you told me that some voice out of the ether told you to read Revelation and afterwards you're convinced it's actually a Hebrew book even though it has been the property of the Church for two thousand years. Following which, you've spent the last few hours trying to convince me that your opinion is correct, even though you knew you'd be attacking some of my core beliefs in the process."

"It wasn't my intention to make you uncomfortable by attacking your beliefs," I spoke up in defense of myself.

"Whether it was your intention or not, that's what you did. And it was mighty uncomfortable. I'm a traditional Catholic and you knew that."

"I told you; I have no recollection of even calling you. At the time I was listening to the voice and as I said, it was as if I was in a trance. Maybe I did call you when I was in that state of mind. I don't really know. But if I did, I have no apologies. We need to get this book published and we need to do it now."

"Well, you did, and I flew over here as soon as possible because of it."

"And as I said, if I did call, then I'm also glad that you came. The thoughts racing around my head were too much already to keep contained. I needed an outlet; and as usual, you were able to provide me with that."

"I know I work for your publisher, but am I just a sounding board that you can use anytime in order to vent your spleen and bounce ideas off of?" Pearce was mad, feeling somewhat used.

"You've always been the one I turned to when it came time to publish my books. And it's always been the company you work for that's done the publishing. So even if my brain was on automatic speed dial to call you, and I just don't recall doing so, then the bottom line is still that I would have called you either way to say that I'm ready to release a new book."

"But then you made me sit here while you repeatedly attacked my faith."

"You know who I am. You know my stories don't always agree with your personal beliefs. We always go through my stories before we release them. This time was no different."

"It was!" Pearce exclaimed. "This time your book I felt was intended to take a direct shot at my beliefs and perhaps even ridicule me."

"I told you that I wasn't attacking your beliefs. And after all our years together, I would never go out of my way to ridicule you. I have no issues in the way you choose to believe in Jesus. You believe he's the son of God, and if that's what you want to believe, then so be it. But I choose not to believe he was anything other than a man who had a very important message for mankind. You need to accept that, as much as you want me to accept you having your beliefs."

"But now you're trying to strip a core book from the New Testament, and I perceive that as an attack on my faith."

"Hey, Revelation was a prophecy on the End of Days. It's not a testimony on Jesus and it is totally unrelated to the Gospels or the letters. The End of Days is not exactly limited to just Christian believers, because if it does come about, then all of us are affected and in deep, deep trouble. So, don't bother trying to put your stamp of ownership on massive misery that will kill hundreds of millions. And should I be wrong about my interpretation, and the hundred and forty-four thousand that get air lifted out of here, and they just happen to be only Christians and you're one of them, then I would be very happy for you John. But still, I'd prefer to battle it out down here because someone has to take a stand and fight against evil. I'm not about to run away from the good fight!"

"I wasn't intending to imply that you were anti-Christian Doc, or anything like that."

"Yes, you were," I corrected him. "But that's okay. You know I don't worship God in the same way you do but ultimately, we worship the same God. We both end up following the same path to righteousness. We share the same moral cause. And side by side, we fight the same battles against the evil of this world."

"If it doesn't make that much of a difference, then why are you trying so hard to claim the book as part of a Hebrew heritage that originally didn't make any references to Jesus. What's the big difference if people still accept it as a Christian manuscript?"

"Because the Christian approach has taken what should have been a very serious prophetic book about our time and turned it into a literal fairy tale. So much so, that it's become a mockery and hardly anyone believes in it. It actually turns away Christian followers because of all its talk of dragons, beasts and armies of angels and demons. Marvel comic book heroes have become more believable. And that's why I think I was told I had to intercede and restore the book to its roots."

"Even if it was a Hebrew book, how's that make a difference?" Pearce still couldn't grasp my point.

"Hebraic Apocrypha are intended to be interpreted metaphorically and not literally. That's why Jews and others can read Isaiah, Ezekiel, Zechariah and Daniel and they know that the supernatural events being described are to be deciphered and the real-world parallels are to be identified. The suffering servant, which was much like a parable from Jesus, for five hundred years was seen as a metaphor for the nation of Israel. A people that God said he loved but which was made to suffer the scourges of every nation, over and over again. But then Christianity comes along and twisted Isaiah's words, claiming that he was describing Jesus Christ, all along. Why, because

Christianity has this obsession of reading prophecies in black and white and therefore everything that it says in your New Testament must be true. Go read my book **The Caiaphas Letters** over again, and you'll see how wrong that assumption is. Did you ever wonder why there are more people believing in the prophecies of Nostradamus than in your Christian tribulation and final battle stories? Because Nostradamus admitted right from the start that his quatrains were metaphors that required interpretations that resided in the physical world. And everyone respects that and marvels that he can talk about the twin giants that fell down at the coordinates of New York, when he couldn't even imagine that man would be able to build structures like the twin towers in Manhattan. That is the purpose of a true prophet and why Christianity needs to rid itself of the influences it absorbed from the pagan religions and rid itself of the beliefs in alternate realms and warring gods."

"Ouch," was Pearce's only response.

"And that's why I believe I was being told to unveil the true history behind the Book of Revelation. It was my purpose to resuscitate its life force and bring it back into the realm in which we live and make people recognize it is a factual commentary on our present civilization, and we are standing at the precipice."

"Maybe there is some credence to what you have to say," Pearce said somewhat apologetically.

Smiling, I responded, "I'm not here to change the words of Jochanan, I am here to reinforce them." I borrowed one of Jesus's more famous phrases regarding the Laws of Moses.

"Now that could be considered somewhat blasphemous," Pearce joked.

"Seriously though, we need people to pay attention to the book and hopefully put down their current version and find a copy of the Aramaic Peshitta that has been translated. Only then will they have a better understanding of the dangers that await us if we don't manage to change the direction we are heading."

"Then you must be rejoicing with the results of the American election in November."

"It's an opportunity to change the direction but one doesn't need to look hard to see the divisiveness and degree of anarchy that permeates American society. Half the country still doesn't want to hear the words of someone like Donald Trump, and it will do anything in order silence him. Those liberties and freedoms that once were the cornerstone of American society have been replaced by self-serving elements of the non-enfranchised and the radicals that seek any opportunity to destroy the democracy which has protected so many in the past. He's got a high hill to climb."

"But if he does so, then there is a chance of restoring peace in the world," Pearce was quick to point out.

"That 'if' is a very powerful word. Even if he does bring about peace in the Ukraine and the Middle East, how long will it last after he leaves office in four years. If the people in America do start seeing eye to eye, how long until one of them pokes the other in the eye and their squabbling begins all over again? If China and America can arrive at a mutual agreement on sharing the economic wealth of the world, how long until one side decides it wants to dominate the other? If radical Islam can be restrained and the more moderate Muslims agree to settle their differences with the rest of the world and we can all sit at the table as cousins, if not brothers, how long until that cancer that resides within the fundamentalist ideology begins to spread again amongst those that believe in theocracies and religious domination?"

"Wasn't it you that believed we could stop the prophecy from being fulfilled and the world as we know it could be saved."

"It can be stopped, prophecies don't necessarily have to come to pass, but I never gave you a statistical probability."

"What do you think he odds are then?"

"Well, if you ask Chat-GPT what the odds of success are for the Donald Trump presidency to end the war in the Ukraine and the Middle East, it provides you with this answer; *The odds of success depend heavily on the willingness of all parties to negotiate and the geopolitical dynamics at the time. While some believe his "unpredictability" could be advantageous, others view his approach as risky and potentially destabilizing.'* As of now, I don't believe the parties are that willing to negotiate. Too much bad blood has been spilled and the rewards that would have to be given to all parties involved would never be seen as equitable or enough by the opposing forces. That being the case, the odds don't appear to be any higher than fifty-fifty."

"I was hoping you were right, and the End of Days could be avoided but those odds aren't particularly heart-warming."

"Better than the last administration. That one had only one outcome and that was to push all the nations into the final battle. Wars have a natural order to follow. It's like playing chess. In order to end the game, either the white or black king has to be removed from the board. Otherwise, you have a stalemate, which means you have to start the game all over again until there is an eventual winner."

"Then you're saying the prophecy has to be fulfilled," Pearce sounded concerned.

"Is any prophecy incontrovertible? I don't believe so. Otherwise, why would the Almighty send us prophets if it wasn't to provide us with the opportunity to change future possibilities. I told you, I'm an optimist. I have to believe no matter how unlikely it may be to stop this prophecy, that there's still a chance it can be done."

"Will we be able to do so?"

"That my friend is the million-dollar question. It's not for me to answer. The decision has to come from all the people in the world. They are the only ones that can guarantee the outcome either way."

EPILOGUE

For those that are interested in learning more about the striking differences between the Aramaic Peshitta and the Textus Receptus, then probably the most noticeable difference is the lack or reduction in direct references to Jesus in the Peshitta version of Revelation. Typically, the older the version of the Peshitta, the lower the number of any references to Jesus, which would suggest that the original manuscript the Peshitta was transcribing, in all likelihood made no references to Jesus, Christ or the Lamb of God at all. This phenomenon raises important questions about the theological and textual history of the Peshitta.

As I just stated the focus of the Peshitta is on God's sovereignty only. The Peshitta often emphasizes the sovereignty of God (YHWH) rather than explicitly naming Jesus in certain passages. Christian theologians have responded to the absence by saying it does not imply a diminished role for Jesus but rather reflects a theological tradition that views Jesus' mission as fully integrated with the divine will. For example, titles such as "Lamb" or "Son of Man" may appear less frequently, but their underlying Christological significance remains intact. As discussed in the Book of Lazarus, the Son of Man has a specific Hebraic meaning, and references to the lamb, as indicated by Isaiah can be pointing at the Children of Israel and not a specific person. Another common statement by the clergy is what they refer to as Implicit Christology. This catch phrase implies that the absence of references to Jesus in the Peshitta, should be taken as being implicit, relying on context and shared understanding within the early Christian community that it is about Jesus, even though he is not mentioned. If this were true, then it certainly contrasts with the Greek tradition, which makes Christological references repeatedly, claiming that it adds doctrinal clarity. To suggest that the Peshitta didn't require the same doctrinal clarity seems somewhat ludicrous and a contradiction of their expert opinion.

The doctrinal clarifications in the Greek Textus Receptus is noted and recognized to often include expanded titles and phrases that explicitly identify Jesus in ways that may reflect doctrinal developments rather than original textual content. For example, the phrase "Jesus Christ" might appear in places where the Peshitta simply uses "the Lord" but not only is this an admission that the clergy deliberately altered and adulterated the original texts but overlooks Hebraic tradition not to mention the name of God, 'Yahweh', and instead substitutes the word Lord.

Liturgical adaptations is another excuse by the Church for their editing of Revelation, by which they claim that some expansions in the Greek text may have been influenced by liturgical use, where explicit references to Jesus were added to align with worship practices. This is a crucial admission that originally the book did not align with Christian practices and changes had to be made so that it would do so.

I've already mentioned scribal tendencies, whether they were deliberate or not, but we all have our personal agendas and the clergy are no different. Avoidance of Redundancy is one of the Church's explanations for the Peshitta lacking references to Jesus in which they suggest that the Aramaic scribes may have deliberately avoided repetitive references to Jesus, assuming the reader would understand the text's Christological implications. A better interpretation based on other ancient texts is that if it isn't included then it was never there in the first place. Church scribes that were taught to exalt in Jesus's name whenever they could, to deliberately avoid mentioning Jesus and consciously doing so, is an explanation not even worth consideration. It is contrary to the entire proselytizing approach of the early church.

Ancient Jewish scholars relied heavily on oral tradition. Prior to the introduction of the Talmud, the entire practice of Jewish tradition relied heavily on oral teaching. It is likely that the Peshitta's more concise references or lack of them is due to its transmission originally through an oral culture, and therefore when it was finally put into writing, it only recorded that which was said in the oral tradition at that time without any additions.. In an effort to deal with the possibility of the accuracy of oral tradition, one can hear the statement from Church scholars that the differences between the Peshitta and the Textus Receptus highlight the dynamic nature of biblical transmission and the interplay between language, culture, and theology. Understanding these differences can deepen our appreciation for the diversity within the early Christian textual tradition and help us approach Revelation with greater nuance. I suggest it does the opposite by emphasizing the early reliance of the Church on Jewish literature and its adopting of some of that literature as its own through the marked effort of rewriting the literature and introducing a purely Christian context and content.

It is important for all denominations to recognize the role of translation in shaping theology over time. Each translation of Revelation reflects the theological priorities and cultural context of its community. The Peshitta's Aramaic background offers a unique lens that can enrich our understanding of Revelation's message because the prophecy can be viewed without the heavy overlay of Christian doctrine, rendering it more universal and therefore a prophetic discourse for more religious people than just those belonging to the Christian faith. .

One can conclude that the differences between the Peshitta and the Textus Receptus underscore the importance of textual criticism in reconstructing the most accurate text of the original Revelation. By comparing these versions, it is my intention that the underlying Jewish apocryphal manuscript can be recognized and as such, its message can become more universal, having a world-wide impact. In that case, what may have been rejected because of its Christian exclusiveness and imagery that leaned heavily on the supernatural, rendering it as too fantastic to be anything other than a Hollywood Sci-Fi movie, can be reviewed more seriously and like other Jewish apocrypha can be deciphered and applied to our current political and economic situation. By now, all readers of the Book of Lazarus should recognize that the Aramaic

Peshitta version of Revelation offers a far more compelling and potentially more accurate rendering of the original text as compared to the Greek Textus Receptus. Its linguistic and cultural proximity to the world of Roman dominated Judea, along with its textual simplicity and alignment with early Jewish manuscript traditions, make it an invaluable resource for biblical scholars and theologians of both Jewish and Christian practices. The lack of explicit references to Jesus in the Peshitta reflect that it had an entirely different theological emphasis, one that integrates anyone with a faith in God into the broader framework of divine sovereignty and the Judeo-Christian heritage. These differences provide rich material for understanding the complex history of Judaism, and how the Hebraic monotheism experienced a varied reception into different Christian communities.

150